OVERCOMING
PROCRASTINATION

OVERCOMING PROCRASTINATION

Do not wait. Grow by Doing.

TERENCE MURINGISI

Posterity Publishing
'Creative Impressions For Posterity'

www.terencemuringisi.org

POSTERITY PUBLISHING

Published by Posterity Publishing. Posterity Publishing, a division of Posterity Media (Private Limited), Harare, Zimbabwe.

ISBN: 978-0-7974-5788-1

CONTENTS

DEDICATION

To our three bubbly babies, Gabriella, John-Buddy and Isabella, I love you. This is dedicated to you as part of the work I have done on your behalf to justify my nearly three decade head start on life.

This is for you, your generation, mine and those to follow. May we fulfill our calling and please our Heavenly Father.

As I concluded the preparation of this book for printing, I received a miraculous and gracious gift from God. I was reunited with my mother, after three decades of separation. I add this special dedication to you mum, to signify the importance of making prompt use of our opportunities, especially with the relationships that we are granted to enjoy.

ACKNOWLEDGMENTS

Our knowledge in the Word of God is the sum total of the inspiration of the Holy Spirit and the work of all our teachers and mentors.

I praise God for and acknowledge all my teachers, too numerous to mention. However, a special thank you for all the encouragement I received to publish from one of my teachers and mentors, Pastor Walter Senah, a published author himself.

Many thanks to Pastors Fridah Murandu and Joseph Mushonga for the diligent editorial feedback provided.

A special acknowledgment to my wife Sarah, I love you and thank you! You have been a great support for me to fulfill what the Heavenly Father placed on my heart to do.

Finally, thank you to a man with an infectious pleasantness and a big heart for potential. My pastor since I was born again and my first human inspiration to preach, Bishop G.S Chigwada.

PREFACE

"This book is a call to action because God fires you with a dream so that you can rise up and do what you saw!"

I was born again or converted to the Christian faith a little over twelve years ago. For about eight years of those twelve, I have served believers in a leadership and teaching capacity, helping others to grow as I grew in faith.

Everything I teach in this book is based on the teachings of the Holy Bible, which I consider to be the very Word and thoughts of God communicated to different men in different places and generations through the Holy Spirit.

I believe that God's Holy Spirit lives in me because of my faith and teaches me all I need to learn regarding life and godliness. This book is meant for all people, believers and non-believers. However, its holistic goals will only be met when the Christian Holy book, The Bible and its implications on human life are believed and trusted. This means that the contents of this book are faith based. You will need to be a person of faith to receive a complete benefit.

Due to my orientation of faith, I will liberally use the names "God," "Holy Spirit," "Jesus Christ," "Prayer" and other biblical references. I will take these terms as accepted for ease of communication. This means I will make only limited effort to explain these terms as any further involvement would cause a detour from the specific objectives of this book.

The second chapter, *"The Most Important, Most Urgent Message in the World"* is for you to begin with if you are not born again. To be born again is to receive new and eternal life by believing and trusting the word of God to be cleansed from sin and reconciled to a righteous relationship with the one God through faith in the sacrifice of His Son Jesus Christ. The chapter is dedicated to show you how you can establish this relationship. Go there now if you are unsure of the status of your relationship with God.

The Holy Spirit taught me the title of this book and other related concepts through a creative play on the letter "P." I began to see that there are several principles that God has given in His word to guide us into a place of success. Many of these principles may be rendered through the use of words beginning with the letter "P."

I have termed these subjects, *"The Ps of Prosperity and Poverty, Success and Failure."* Their purpose is to identify and deal with several factors that hinder or promote God ordained success and welfare in the lives of believers. "Procrastination" is one of those factors that hinder this success.

The subject of "Procrastination" is the dedication of this particular book, a subject that has become the first "P." We will define this word then delve into the chapters.

Procrastination is the:

Counterproductive delay or postponement of the performance of necessary, higher priority tasks or assignments in favour of lower priority ones.

This may be put simply as *"postponing the needful for the needless."*

I have decided to write about it because I am no stranger to the vice. I know about being full of good intentions and little done. Writing this book is a kind of me serving immediate divorce papers on the vice. It is my quintessential breaking of ties with mediocre behaviour or association.

Recently and quite painfully, I learnt through an informal chat with a colleague that *"...good intentions are cheap."* That statement hit me hard as I spoke to them but I kept cool and straight-faced, not wanting to give anything away. They had touched a subject of my present passion, to see me and others set off on a path of victory over delay. If *"...good intentions are cheap"* was a blow to the bowels that bent me over in agony, they soon followed it with a swift jab to the chin.

"Life has to be organised, otherwise you can look good but going nowhere..." they added, pulling no punches. Well, just to be clear, there was no malice in their speech. We were having a cordial discussion about a business project and they were merely painting the picture that *"solution givers are doers."* They referred to how it is a travesty that the efforts of one particular man's entrepreneurial vision in our country was feeding over fifty thousand orphans consistently while the rest of us looked on. That is where he remarked, *"...we all want to feed orphans don't we.....but good intentions are cheap."*

I concurred that many may have a good ideal but only a few pay the price to see the ideal materialise. Well, to say *"good intentions are cheap"* is not entirely true because God does value a good heart and good thoughts, intentions and desires. Many have an evil and selfish agenda in their hearts and so the ones who have intentions that God can assess as *"good"* have excelled many of their peers in the sight of God.

However, what we can take out from it is that good intentions are certainly of lesser value than action.

This is the premise of this book, to see you overcome the factors that fetter the feet and bind the hands from action. It is a blow to the bowels and a jab to the chin to wake you up from the drowsiness of laziness that clothes a man with rags. This book is a call to action because God fires you with a dream so that you can rise up and do what you saw!

"PROCRASTINATION IS THE NUMBER ONE "P" BECAUSE WE CANNOT AFFORD TO DELAY TALKING ABOUT DELAY"

1.

WISDOM

To begin with, let us reiterate the simplified definition of "Procrastination." It is:

Postponing the needful for the needless

Procrastination leads to the delay of outcomes which bring productivity, blessing and add value to ourselves and those around us. We need to discover what causes us to delay the performance of those things which are necessary for our progress and success.

Having identified these causes, we must deliberately exclude them from our lives. In their place, we must include those thoughts, decisions and behaviours that cause us to be prompt performers of what we are called to do.

I implore you therefore, brothers, by the mercies of God, that you present your bodies a living sacrifice, holy, acceptable unto God, which is your reasonable service. And do not be conformed to this world: but be transformed by the renewing of your mind, that you may prove what is that good, and acceptable, and perfect, will of God. (Romans 12v1-2)

The word of God is the authority that we will use as the standard for us to overcome this "P." The word is the power that renews our minds so that our behaviours may change. The change of our behaviour will result in the outcome of our lives in victory over delay. Once we have obtained the truth of the word, two choices are before us, wisdom or foolishness.

Therefore whosoever hears these sayings of mine, and does them, I will liken him unto a wise man, which built his house upon a rock:

And every one that hears these sayings of mine, and does not do them, shall be likened unto a foolish man, which built his house upon the sand: (Matthew 7:24,26)

In the record of Matthew, the Lord Jesus Christ defined wisdom as hearing his words and doing them. On the contrary, foolishness was outlined as hearing and not doing. After learning anything in life, it is a change in behaviour which results in success. We can hear all we want, but if we do not change, our lives are not any better for what we have heard.

Wisdom is the principal thing; therefore get wisdom: and with all your getting, get understanding (Proverbs 4:7)

"Principal" means major, most important, foremost or chief. This is the place of wisdom in our lives.

Wisdom is so important that the scriptures urge us to pursue it. We are encouraged to "get wisdom" as the top priority, the most important, chief and foremost pursuit of our lives.

Happy is the man that finds wisdom, and the man that gets understanding. For the merchandise of it is better than the merchandise of silver, and the gain thereof than fine gold. She is more precious than rubies: and all the things you can desire are not to be compared unto her. Length of days is in her right hand; and in her left hand riches and honour. (Proverbs 3v13-16)

We do not find anywhere that the scriptures urge us to "get rich" or to "be successful." We are urged to pursue wisdom. Grasping wisdom assures us of every other blessing of life. Success, wealth and long life are all the fruits of wisdom. Wisdom must be obtained *first* and the rest will *follow*.

Interestingly, as I began to write about wisdom in this section, I wondered about writing *"The Principal Thing" (Wisdom)* as the first "P" of Prosperity and Poverty instead of "Procrastination." *"After all, Wisdom is the principal thing..."* I thought. *"Where else can one start but with the first and foremost thing?"* Then I thought to myself, *"that would be unwise, because we cannot afford to delay talking about delay..."* The *application* of wisdom demanded that a handling of the subject of Procrastination, which is delay come before a mere *discussion* about wisdom (the principal thing).

Applying wisdom is clearly better than talking about it. In writing on this series, one of the ways I applied wisdom is to choose application over discussion.

The next chapters are dedicated to the detail of the wisdom of God in overcoming delay. In another New Testament text, the Apostle Paul deals with the subject of time in a way that lends some more insight into the relationship between wisdom and victory over delay.

> *Look carefully then how you walk, not as unwise but as wise, making the best use of the time, because the days are evil. Therefore do not be foolish, but understand what the will of the Lord is. And do not get drunk with wine, for that is debauchery, but be filled with the Spirit, (Ephesians 5:15-18)*

In writing to the church at Ephesus, Paul encourages them to be vigilant about their lives. He warns them not to be fools but to be wise. The encouragement is given to us too in our day.

What he refers to as "wisdom" in this context may be interpreted from what he mentions before and after this call to wisdom. This is what he says before and after the words "*...not as unwise but as wise...*" in the quoted verses. In other words, what he says before and after that phrase is the way to walk in wisdom.

This is remarkable and is listed here to show some of the factors that must be attended to as part of the wisdom to overcome procrastination. We would like to ensure that our work in this book expands these factors to show us the way to do things promptly. On completing this book, you should be able to review the list and see how the contents of this book have helped you to obey each one of these factors and more. I say *"and more"* because our discourse will not be limited to this list.

1. *Pay attention to how you live your life*
2. *Make the best use of your time*
3. *Understand the will of God*
4. *Do not be ill disciplined or reckless*
5. *Be filled with the Spirit*
6. *Remember that the times are evil*

These factors may be presented as foundational for our entire argument in this book. In the pages to the end of this book, we explore and expand several topics that seek to achieve what the writer encourages in those verses of *Ephesians Chapter 5*. In those few lines, he discourages foolishness and encourages wisdom.

Key among the six aspects which Paul touches on in encouraging wisdom instead of foolishness is the age old principle of the management of time. He urges us, *"make the best use of your time..."*

Another version of the Bible renders the same statement *"redeeming the time..."* To redeem the time is to make up for lost time. It is to make every effort to maximise on the time made available to employ it for its best and most appropriate use. You may have wasted time before you got hold of this book and learnt something. I urge you to make up your mind to make up for lost time by exercising wisdom from now on.

So teach us to number our days, that we may apply our hearts unto wisdom (Psalm 90:12)

In this Psalm, the writer catches our attention through a most solemn subject matter. We are on this earth for a limited time. We are not here forever. Most of us will see death in the earth. The only ones excluded are those that will still be alive when the Lord Jesus Christ returns in the clouds and shall be caught up together with him and forever be with Him. This is as spoken in the book of *1st Thessalonians.*

For the Lord himself shall descend from heaven with a shout, with the voice of the archangel, and with the trump of God: and the dead in Christ shall rise first: Then we which are alive and remain shall be caught up together with them in the clouds, to meet the Lord in the air: and so shall we ever be with the Lord. Therefore comfort one another with these words. (1Thessalonians 4v16-18)

What does it mean to *"number our days"*? It means to carefully consider, take stock, reckon or keep accounts of your days of life. It also refers to understanding that you are not in the earth forever. This makes the time resource definite or *"defined within finite limits"* as opposed to *"unlimited to infinity."*

You see, we are naturally always careful with those things that are scarce or in limited supply and generally careless with the abundant. Wisdom is the fitting response of human behaviour to a limited resource. As a result, the Psalmist draws our attention to the length of our days in the earth. Our days are not forever. The fitting response to this reality is wisdom.

The application of wisdom and *"making the best use of our time"* is generally difficult to do because time is generally perceived as an abundant thing. It is this perceived abundance that leads to waste. Water is generally in more abundance than oil. As a result, the petrol attendant is more likely to leave the *water tap* than the *fuel pump* running.

"WISDOM IS THE FITTING RESPONSE OF HUMAN BEHAVIOUR TO A LIMITED RESOURCE."

The first step to overcoming this is to recognize time as a *resource* rather that a *"thing."* Viewing time as a resource changes everything. Resources or assets are the basis of creating value. When you list the resources that you had at your disposal to make or achieve anything, I do not see how you cannot list *time* as one of them. Failure to list time as one of the resources instrumental for you to achieve an outcome will lead you to ignore it in future planning for success. In starting a business, you could successfully project the cash, building, machinery and people you need to be successful but ignore the demand it will have on your time. When either your business, family or other goals begin to suffer, time emerges as a key resource. We only plan for what is important so it is basic for us to recognize time as a resource.

It sometimes takes instruction, preaching or the death of a close acquaintance or relation to emphatically remember *"for a season"* that time is important. We are giving sustained attention to the subject matter in this book to help make this attention more than seasonal.

"WE ONLY PLAN FOR WHAT IS IMPORTANT."

Recognize time as a resource and you will pay attention to it. Remember that it is a resource in limited supply and you will not waste it. Every resource is consumed or used up. You must see how it is that you actually consume time as a resource every day. This is why the Psalmist prays that God would help him *"number"* his days. He was actually asking God to help him recognize time as a resource so that he could *account* for it the way we account for money.

Almost every normal and average person starting out the day

with an amount of money will take some time at the end of the day to consider *what they did with their money*. The above average person will consider *what they will do with their money* before they leave the house. It is the same with time.

Those who coined the term *"Time is money"* may have had the same endeavour we have here in mind, which is *"recognizing time as a resource."* That is a good analogy, however, the things that time can do go well beyond mere money. This makes the analogy limited in that respect.

"RECOGNIZE TIME AS A RESOURCE AND YOU WILL PAY ATTENTION TO IT. REMEMBER THAT IT IS A RESOURCE IN LIMITED SUPPLY AND YOU WILL NOT WASTE IT"

Perhaps we can postulate here that:

Time is a resource which can be harnessed to produce value in various forms.

That said, I am aware, as the coiners of *"Time is money"* probably were that people are generally more familiar with money than any other resource. This makes *"Time is money"* easy to remember and a sufficient analogy to make the point that it is a resource worth valuing. I will employ this analogy to help you remember what you are dealing with whenever you wake up. Imagine that someone credits your bank account with US$24,000 every day. Remember, I said, *"imagine."* I had to remind you before you start looking for your ATM card. As with anything *"unbelievable!"* there are conditions:

Condition 1*: You cannot carry a balance of that gratuity forward into the next day. You can only apply the cash to a purpose of your choice.*

Condition 2: *What you create or convert your cash into, you can keep for as long as it lasts.*

Condition 3: *God will give eternal rewards for expenditure on the causes He cares about.*

Condition 4: *You neither have any idea nor control on the end date of the flow of the daily gratuity. Today's receipt may be the last and you have no way of knowing.*

That sum of money is symbolic of the time you receive daily. Two obvious responses will emerge for almost any person presented with this scenario. It might be:

Spend it all everyday!

With time, that response was taken care of by default.
We actually do *"Spend it all everyday!"* However, a daily choice remains in our control. That is:

Spend it on what?

It is the choices that are made in response to *Spend it on what?* which differentiate people in this life and the next. These choices are wisdom or foolishness. There are a couple of suggestions that may assist you to be *wise* and make a difference.

1. Plan your expenditure in advance
2. Perform your planned expenditure promptly
3. Spend on the causes that God cares about

In other words, wisdom calls upon you not to start a day without a plan. The day's time will run out on you while you are still finding your feet and deciding what to do. Someone with a well planned day does not lose any time to fiddling and guesswork. When you plan, you can get up and get straight to work. Planning is dealt with in detail later but it suffices to note here that it is a tenet of wisdom. The wise do it, why don't you?

Part of the reason why there is so much idling in bed in the mornings, clouded by drowsiness, is a lack of planning. You *cannot* be prompt to hop out of bed and rush to the bathroom, to get ready to do...nothing.

Having a plan, you must be swift to do what you have determined to do. Wisdom acts fast because time does not pause until you have put yourself together. Just like you would spend your money promptly in the scenario outlined above, do what you must quickly so that you do not waste a moment.

Lastly, it is important to consider exactly what you put down on your plan. Prioritize the things that God cares about and you have just become a person of wisdom. The choice remains yours everyday but you are encouraged to choose wisely. When the will of God is known and respected, this is considered the entry point of wisdom.

This is what the scripture means with:

The fear of the Lord is the beginning of all wisdom (Proverbs 9:10)

2.

THE MOST IMPORTANT, MOST URGENT MESSAGE IN THE WORLD

If our days are limited in the earth, we ought to know our focus and dedication. Ignorance in this may result in us spending our limited days in recklessness. We have got to understand what is most important and urgent to know, hear and do. This understanding is indispensable. With just a little bit of time in the morning, we know how to focus on core activities so that we can get to our next appointment on time. It should be the same with life.

Procrastination is costliest in the most important and most urgent matters. Of all the important things to be done in the world, I will be bold to let you know that the word of God has let us know the most important and urgent. Out of the millions of pursuits in the world, the most important and urgent has been identified for us.

In order to grasp the answer, we will need to work on the meaning of *Psalm 90:12* read in the previous chapter.

So teach us to number our days, that we may apply our hearts unto wisdom (Psalm 90:12)

We have already dealt with the phrase, "......*so teach us to number our days*" and would now like to focus our attention on, "...*that we may apply our hearts unto wisdom.*" What is wisdom, beside it being the principal thing? Wisdom is the answer to the question *"How?"* It is a superior kind of knowledge which carries practical ability.

"PROCRASTINATION IS COSTLIEST IN THE MOST IMPORTANT, MOST URGENT MATTERS"

"Knowledge," having answered the question *"What?"* meaning, *"What is to be done?,"* *"Wisdom"* answers the question *"How is it to be done correctly?"* With a limited number of days in the earth, the Psalmist recognized that he had to win in the area of wisdom, this can be broken down into:

1. *Know what to do (Knowledge)*
2. *Know what to do and why (Understanding)*
3. *Do it (Faith)*
4. *Do it the right way (Wisdom)*

I believe that knowledge, understanding and faith are all elements of wisdom. The element of faith is included clearly because the Psalmist said, *"that we may apply..."*
Application, action or works are the only evidence of faith.

But of him are you in Christ Jesus, who of God is made unto us wisdom, and righteousness, and sanctification, and redemption: (1 Corinthians 1:30)

Jesus Christ's advent in the earth is a historical fact. It is only the spiritual implications of His coming that many debate. The Bible, in the text quoted above labours to make known part of these spiritual implications.

The implications in this verse are set out to show how God, the Father made Jesus Christ:

1. *Wisdom*
2. *Righteousness*
3. *Sanctification and*
4. *Redemption*

Jesus Christ is the wisdom of God. If He is the wisdom of God:

What was the question?

For the wages of sin is death; but the gift of God is eternal life through Jesus Christ our Lord. (Romans 6:23)

And the LORD God commanded the man, saying, Of every tree of the garden you may freely eat: But of the tree of the knowledge of good and evil, you shall not eat of it: for in the day that you eat thereof you shall surely die. (Genesis 2:16-17)

The question was the sentence of death that was upon all sinners. The text clearly communicates that the penalty or the reward of sin is death. All men inherited the sinful nature of mind and body through the original sin that Adam, our common forefather committed through disobedience. Remember, God said to Adam, *"...for in the day that you eat thereof you shall surely die."* Death was the sentence for sin.

Who are the sinners?

For all have sinned, and come short of the glory of God (Romans 3:23)

Every human being is a sinner because *all* means *all*.

All of mankind missed the mark of God's standard of righteousness. What does all this mean? It means that there is no human being that can claim to be sinless, that is, without fault or failure to obey the commandments of God. Adam's original sin introduced the nature of sin into the human race. Thereafter, no one born out of the biological seed of a man could escape it. Every man comes to consciousness and sins as a matter of course.

How did Jesus Christ answer this question?

For the wages of sin is death; but the gift of God is eternal life through Jesus Christ our Lord. (Romans 6:23)

For God so loved the world, that he gave his only begotten Son, that whosoever believes in him should not perish, but have everlasting life. (John 3:16)

Jesus answered, Surely, surely, I say unto you, except a man be born of water and of the Spirit, he cannot enter into the kingdom of God.

That which is born of the flesh is flesh; and that which is born of the Spirit is spirit. (John 3:5-6)

Jesus Christ became the gift of God to humanity so that all that believe and trust in His sacrifice on their behalf would not have to receive the penalty of death. Rather, by God's mercy, they would become the heirs of eternal life because of their trusting reliance in the free sacrifice of blood that Jesus Christ paid on their behalf.

The mercy and miracle that God delivered to the human race through Jesus Christ was that all who believe would receive a new life. It would be a new and eternal life received through faith. This is what it means to be born again. It is to put off the old natural life dominated by sin and death through Adam to inherit a new spiritual eternal life through Jesus Christ.

To be born again is a miracle. It is the single most *important* and *urgent* news in the world. I will qualify why this is so.

1. We judge *importance* by the *implications* or *impact* of *doing* or *not doing* a thing
2. We judge *urgency* by the *implications* of the *promptness* or *delay* of the doing of an important thing.

A man's salvation is head and shoulders above any other thing in importance because the implications of not placing reliance on the free gift of God for salvation are eternal. *John 3:16* shows that God's rescue mission through Jesus Christ was to *save* us from *destruction*. Note the scripture says, "*...so that he that believes in Him would not perish...*" That word *perish* is a serious cause for concern.

"TO BE BORN AGAIN IS A MIRACLE. IT IS THE SINGLE MOST IMPORTANT, MOST URGENT NEWS IN THE WORLD!"

The danger of that *perishing* or *destruction* is what makes the gospel of Jesus Christ the most important message in the world. None can compete because *perishing* carries the implication of utter and outright destruction, with no possibility of recovery. It would be enough for the message to rank highest in importance; however, it also ranks highest in urgency.

Jesus Christ did not wait in the heavenly realms to perform His rescue mission. He took the form of mankind and was born as a man in order to rescue us here in the earth. The earth is the arena of decisions which carry eternal implications. Jesus was crucified in the earth. As a result, mankind must also respond to this sinless sacrifice *in the earth*. The earth is the context for all your decisions, of which the decision to respond to the saving act of Jesus Christ in repentance and faith is chief.

"THE EARTH IS THE ARENA OF DECISIONS WHICH CARRY ETERNAL IMPLICATIONS"

Whereas you do not know what shall be tomorrow. For what is your life? It is even a vapour that appears for a little time, and then vanishes away. (James 4:14)

The urgency factor is revealed in that our lives in the earth are likened to the fickle and quick transitory nature of vapour or steam. We are here one moment and the next we are gone. If we knew the time of our departure, urgency would be disqualified, but no one knows the hour of their death. Death comes like a thief, unannounced.

"THE EARTH IS THE CONTEXT FOR ALL YOUR DECISIONS, OF WHICH THE DECISION TO RESPOND TO THE SAVING ACT OF JESUS CHRIST IN REPENTANCE AND FAITH IS CHIEF"

This makes the moment of one's hearing the gospel the very opportunity of their salvation. In that opportunity, the Bible has already encouraged us not to harden our hearts.

While it is said, today if you will hear his voice, harden not your hearts, as in the provocation. (Hebrews 3:15)

The provocation referred to here is the rebellion of much of the children of Israel when Moses led them out of Egypt to the Promised Land. They refused to believe God even though He did many wonderful miracles in their sight. There remained no reason for them not to believe but they chose to be stubborn. This is what it means *"to harden your heart."* You have hardened your heart when a reasonable individual in the same circumstances would have repented. But, alas, you stood tall, proud and strolled away from God's providence.

> *God's anger is shown from heaven against all the evil and wrong things people do. By their own evil lives they hide the truth. God shows his anger because some knowledge of him has been made clear to them. Yes, God has shown himself to them. There are things about him that people cannot see – his eternal power and all the things that make him God. But since the beginning of the world those things have been easy to understand by what God has made. So people have no excuse for the bad things they do. (Romans 1:18 – 20) (New Century Version)*

In our day, we harden our hearts when we refuse to respond to the gospel. We delay and postpone the serious consideration of the truth to a later date. This is a future date that we have no assurance of seeing.

Even though natural creation itself stands on the podium and preaches the existence of God daily, mankind continues to rebel in hardness of heart. There is a refusal to admit that creation itself is testimony of the God of the Holy Bible who has set forth the way of mankind's reconciliation with Himself through Jesus Christ.

The moment of hearing the gospel is not a moment to delay, postpone or procrastinate. It is a time to meditate on the words heard and respond in humility to the message, repenting and calling upon the name of Jesus Christ for salvation from sin and impending death.

There is a clear call to urgency on the part of the one who hears the gospel. This message is not only the most important, but also the most urgent message in the world. What could be more important and urgent than the choice between eternal life or eternal damnation, destruction, contempt and shame?

Before we proceed, I would like to give you an opportunity to act on the gospel of salvation through faith in Jesus Christ. Consider the scriptures we have discussed in this chapter. Here are additional scriptures to help you. Some of them are repeated for your convenience:

John 3:16
John 14:6
Mark 16:15-16 and
Romans 10:9

Talk to God in sincerity, the prayer below is only a guideline.

"Heavenly Father, I thank you for your word. I admit that I have sinned and fallen short of your requirements. I repent of my sins. I believe that Jesus Christ died and rose again to reconcile me to you. I believe that your word says that if I call upon the name of Jesus, I shall be saved."

If you have responded in humility and faith to the discussion above, you have made the most important decision of your life. The rest of your life has begun.

Do not say, there are yet four months, and then comes the harvest?

Behold, I say unto you, Lift up your eyes, and look on the fields; for they are white already to harvest (John 4:35)

In the words above, the Lord Jesus Christ shows that the message of salvation in His name is also of importance and urgency to those who are charged with its dispensation to others.

He urges his disciples not to delay the preaching of the gospel to bring in a harvest of souls. He urges them to look out into the world and observe how the people are ready for this salvation. In summary, He urged His disciples not to wait, postpone, delay or procrastinate.

After all, is it not the most important and most urgent message in the world?

Therefore if any man is in Christ, he is a new creature: old things have passed away; behold, all things have become new. And all things are of God, who has reconciled us to himself by Jesus Christ, and has given to us the ministry of reconciliation. (2 Corinthians 5:17-18)

The message of salvation from sin and death and introduction to eternal life is so important and urgent that everyone who is born again is charged with its immediate dispensation to the entire world. The salvation of Jesus Christ reconciled us back to God, not only that, it then gave into our hands, an urgent assignment to confer that same message of reconciliation to others.

Take a look below at the commission that Jesus gave His disciples and all who should believe through their message. So important and urgent is this assignment that it made it into His parting words:

All authority is given unto me in heaven and in earth. Go therefore, and teach all nations, baptizing them in the name of the Father, and of the Son, and of the Holy Ghost: Teaching them to observe all things whatsoever I have commanded you: and, look, I am with you always, even unto the end of the world. Amen. (Matthew 28:18-20)

Perhaps when His disciples would talk about it later, they would say, *"How important these words are, the words He made sure to speak to us in the days before He left."* We ought to consider the same thing.

3.

YOUR SUCCESS IS GOD'S WILL

It is important to set the foundation by establishing that it is God's will for you to be successful. This sounds obvious but it is not. Some will readily accept this as the truth while many others may struggle to believe it.

Those who struggle to receive this truth are my specific audience in this section. The rest of the book will be of no value without this foundation because procrastination is only a vice worthy of attention to a person who cares about succeeding.

The one who does not care about achieving anything and doing it well has no need to mind the use of their time, nor the effectiveness of their efforts. This person can be reckless, not caring about the outcome of their endeavour.

> **"PROCRASTINATION IS ONLY A
> VICE WORTHY OF ATTENTION
> TO A PERSON WHO CARES
> ABOUT SUCCEEDING"**

One of the main reasons why someone may struggle to accept that success is the will of God is a poor definition of terms. What is success? What is failure? What is prosperity and poverty?

Words mean things, such that when we fail to define words, we obtain the wrong interpretation. When we carry the wrong inter-pretation, we foster the wrong attitude. When we foster the wrong attitude we will give an inappropriate and unwelcoming response to something that was otherwise a blessing.

Only a few non-Christians will have a problem with accepting success as noble. On the other hand, many Christians may have a problem with the subject due to its frequent mishandling and abuse in the various Bible teaching platforms of the world.

The impact of this is far-reaching. Due to theological or doctrinal misinterpretation, many may maintain an attitude of disdain for that which God intends. The outcome is a denial of God ordained progress and accomplishment which fulfils the plans of God.

The desire for success is a natural human inclination that God does not take away when a man is born again, rather redirecting, informing and tampering it for His glory.

Let us define some terms. In common, day to day use:

1. *Success is achieving the proper outcome as it was intended and*
2. *Prosperity is the possession of "riches," "wealth" and "material things" in abundance.*

Please take note that these are not my definitions but are the most prevalent everyday use.

Let us take a look at my definitions as interpreted from scrip-tures which we shall review later:

1. *Success is making progress at achieving what God has intended.*
2. *Prosperity is a state of total well-being of spirit, soul and body including having access to sufficient material resources to do God's will.*
3. *Failure is the inability to fulfill the objectives God has intended.*
4. *Poverty is a state of lack in spirit, soul and body including not having access to sufficient resources to fulfill the will of God for your life.*

From the above definitions, we will show:

1. How God wants His people to be successful, to do well, to be well and to overcome in life
2. How success and prosperity are not limited to material or financial abundance
3. How an individual can be successful by God's definition but not wealthy by earthly or common use standards.

As touched on before, there is a good reason why we will talk about success when the subject matter is procrastination. It is a necessary subject because there is no motivation to overcome procrastination for an individual who does not care about achieving something. That said, this chapter will also deal with material things, riches or wealth because success and money are often associated.

God wants His people to be successful, to do well, to be well and to overcome in life.

The case for this truth may be made through various extents of labour in the word. For our purposes in this work, we hope to establish this truth as accepted by presenting a couple of scriptures which I believe will give us enough to work with in order to place *"Overcoming Procrastination"* in appropriate context.

In the beginning God created the heaven and the earth. And the earth was without form, and void; and darkness was upon the face of the deep. And the Spirit of God moved upon the face of the waters. And God said, Let there be light: and there was light. And God saw the light, that it was good: and God divided the light from the darkness. (Genesis 1:1-4)

God wants you to be successful at what you do. It is counter-intuitive to believe otherwise. Why would God design you for failure? How could one who himself has not and does not fail design you and I for it? He assessed his own work severally and came out with the opinion *"it was good."*

Let us just consider ourselves for a moment. Those of us with children know how we watch with bated breath when they attempt to do one thing or the other for the first time. This is true for the first step, first climb or whatsoever positive thing they attempt to do. Our hearts leap with excitement as we urge them on to do it *successfully!*

Show me one parent who is wishing their child to miss as they wobble up to kick the ball. You can almost kick it for them so that you can enjoy the satisfaction of seeing their wide grin and giggles at their *"accomplishment."*

It is the same with every other virtuous endeavour our children attempt. We are over 100% behind them to do it well. If you do not have children, it is the same with every close relationship. The natural human inclination is the success of those that are dear. This is part of the *"natural affection"* that Paul speaks of and laments that in the last days many shall be *"...without natural affection..."* *(Romans 1:31 and 2 Timothy 3:3).* Through the Holy Spirit, he saw a day when mankind would become so evil; they would lose the natural tendencies embodied into the created human nature. One of these *natural affections* is this desire for the welfare and success of loved ones.

If we are made this way as people, is it not an obvious matter that God desires you and I to be successful?

Could we be more virtuous than God, desiring our children and relatives well while God wishes us to remain in some state of languishing or failure? This cannot be. Listen to what God says to Joshua as he commissions Him to take over from his predecessor Moses:

> *This book of the law shall not depart out of your mouth; but you shall meditate in it day and night, that you may observe to do according to all that is written in it: for then you shall make your way prosperous, and then you shall have good success. (Joshua 1:8)*

Joshua is given *instructions for success* in the above text. He is told to keep the word of God in his speech and meditation. The result of this kind of focus on the word of God is that he would be able to pay attention to behave and act in accordance with what it says. The final outcome of Joshua's obedience is made clear in that he would discover prosperity and success in his life.

Now, was this outcome of prosperity and success God's will for Joshua's life? Certainly, otherwise God would not have been careful to show and command him to keep the disciplines that would get him there. It is clear that God intended prosperity and success for Joshua.

Was it for Joshua alone? No, it is for you and I too.

Look at the very first Psalm below:

Blessed is the man that does not walk in the counsel of the ungodly, nor stand in the way of sinners, nor sit in the seat of the scornful. But his delight is in the law of the LORD; and in his law he meditates day and night. And he shall be like a tree planted by the rivers of water, that brings forth his fruit in his season; his leaf also shall not wither; and whatsoever he does shall prosper. The ungodly are not so: but are like the chaff which the wind drives away. Therefore the ungodly shall not stand in the judgment, nor sinners in the congregation of the righteous. For the LORD knows the way of the righteous: but the way of the ungodly shall perish. (Psalm 1:1-6)

The very first line shows that the wisdom of God that follows is for all! I am glad that I see it say *"Blessed is the man...."* That means you and I are the focus for the wisdom that follows as listed:

1. *Do not walk in ungodly advice*
2. *Do not follow the lifestyles of sinners*
3. *Do not copy those who mock the things of God*
4. *Love the word of God*
5. *Meditate in the word of God continually*

You are also a candidate for the following rewards of obeying the wisdom listed above:

1. *Strength and stability like a tree*
2. *Continual fruitfulness*
3. *Prosperity in whatsoever you do*

Again, as in Joshua's case, God prescribes the wisdom that should be followed in order to see an outcome of rewards. Part of that outcome is success in one's activities. What doubt do you have left that God's intention is unambiguous regarding your success?

In both instances, that is, Joshua's and *Psalm Chapter 1*, God prescribes a focus on the word of God as the recipe for this success. The word of God is His *"Will."* It is like a man who dies and leaves the allocation of his estate documented for those who remain to administer it in accordance with his desires.

We learn here that it is in doing God's will that one may find success. Success is not doing *"anything"* well. It is doing what God intends well. You can only discover what God intends by paying attention to God's word.

This is the basis for our definition of success given at the beginning of this chapter. We will render it here again as a reminder:

Success is making progress at achieving what God has intended.

Add to this the words of John to the believers below:

*Beloved, I wish above all things that you may prosper and be
in health, even as your soul prospers. (3 John 1:2)*

Is it possible that John, a man could be more benevolent than God? Could he desire the welfare and good of the people more than God? Certainly not! John indeed expressed his personal desire for the health and prosperity of the people. However, his will was so intertwined with the will of God, that those words are the word of God.

All scripture is given by the inspiration of the Holy Spirit and here, John's desire for the prosperity of the people cannot be divorced from God's own personal desire. It certainly was God's will spoken through John.

Only the one who has settled it in mind and heart that success is the will of God will be motivated to overcome a vice like procrastination, delay or postponement. The one who does not care about success has no objectives to aim for and do well. The one with no objectives or goals is going nowhere because you cannot go nowhere or aim at nothing. Faith is the substance of goals. No goals, no faith!

Success and prosperity are not limited to material or financial abundance

The will of God is the key. The will of God as outlined in His word is the purpose of humanity. Doing it well is success! You see how it is clear that you cannot limit success and prosperity to material abundance?

There are many in this world that possess abundance of things. This is neither success nor prosperity by God's definition. This is merely being rich and "rich" is also worthy of definition. It would be more apt and concise to say, *"This is merely being rich in this world."*

The only merit in being rich in this world is that it is proof of:

The successful harnessing, manipulation and dominion of the systems of this world to profit.

The above can be done with or without a relationship with God. In addition, it can also be done either by honest or dishonest means. That said, riches are neither the evidence of godliness nor ungodliness. A person may be rich in goods and yet out of favour with God or without them and yet full of favour.

Let us look at this story that the Lord Jesus Christ told to teach regarding material or financial riches:

And he spoke a parable to them, saying, the ground of a certain rich man brought forth plentifully: And he thought within

27

himself, saying, what shall I do, because I have no room where to store my fruits? And he said, this will I do: I will pull down my barns, and build greater; and there will I store all my fruits and my goods. And I will say to my soul, Soul, you have much goods laid up for many years; take your ease, eat, drink, and be merry. But God said unto him, you fool, this night your soul shall be required of you: then whose shall those things be, which you have provided? So is he that lays up treasure for himself, and is not rich toward God. (Luke 12:16-21)

This is a very interesting story and very much like the wisdom of our Lord to show us that a man can be *"rich"* and *"a fool"* at the same time. To begin with, this man's status in this world was clear. He was rich. He had an abundance of goods and he knew it. He accounted for what he owned in abundance to the extent that he decided to extend his storage capacity.

There was nothing foolish or evil about his riches.

Money does some necessary and beneficial things in the earth. The Lord Jesus Christ did not infer that his folly was in his possession of riches. The Lord Jesus identifies the folly in the last verse: *"...So is he that lays up treasure for himself, and is not rich toward God." (verse 21)*.

In other words, that last verse means, *"In the same way, the one who stores up treasure for himself and yet is not rich toward God is a fool."* The man's foolishness was the confidence he placed in his stored riches while he was bankrupt toward God.

But seek first the kingdom of God, and his righteousness; and all these things shall be added unto you. (Matthew 6:33)

Let us buttress our point by showing that the principal pursuit of our lives should be *"The Kingdom of God"* and *"...His righteousness"* and not material things. In other words, the Kingdom of God is the priority of life. Every other pursuit in life is secondary to the pursuit of the kingdom of God and His righteousness.

The kingdom of God is God's realm of ruler-ship. It is God ruling according to His will. The will of God is the word of God.

Where-ever the word of God is allowed to rule and is accepted; the kingdom of God has made its home in that place.

The righteousness of God is being in right standing with God in the condition of the heart. This is with your thoughts, words and actions in alignment with that heart condition.

If the Kingdom of God should be the principal pursuit of life, it means that there is disorder in a life that has grasped secondary pursuits in its place. This was the condition of the *"Rich man."* He had focused on and acquired riches in this world but did not possess the kingdom of God.

The grasping of the kingdom of God is the priority of pursuit. It is the number one thing for which every person in this world should reach for. Clearly then, it is the first and foremost thing concerning which procrastination should be defeated. Does it not make sense to do first that which is most important? Did not the Lord Jesus say *"seek first the Kingdom of God and His righteousness....."*? All delay and postponement regarding the pursuit of the things of the Kingdom of God should be overcome. This was the point of the prior chapter, *"The Most Important, Most Urgent Message In The World."* That chapter showed how to enter into that Kingdom without delay.

Finding and entering the realm where God rules is the first priority for your life. With that realm, you must find His righteousness. This is why to be merely rich materially or financially is not success or prosperity. If the pursuit of the kingdom of God and His righteousness is our focus, the second part of the quoted verse is God's.

We are called to pursue Him as a priority while he adds material to meet our needs. The first part is *our* focus, the second is *His*. This should not be vice versa. We are labouring the point that success is the accomplishing of the goals that God intends. This is an awareness of the will of God and an eagerness to do it, according to its schedule and to the required specifications. Again, this discussion is fundamental to the subject matter of this book because to overcome procrastination through God's power, you must desire success by God's definition. This is not empty, bankrupt ambition

29

to gather goods and accolades in this world. It is a godly desire to do God's will. Doing God's will according to His specifications is success!

"TO OVERCOME PROCRASTINATION THROUGH GOD'S POWER, YOU MUST DESIRE SUCCESS BY GOD'S DEFINITION."

God will meet your needs

In *Psalm 23:1*, the Psalmist said *"The Lord is my shepherd, I shall not want."* When you follow God's will to do it, there is the guarantee of sufficiency. God has promised that He will meet the basic needs of all His children. This is the principle that the Lord Jesus Christ taught below:

Therefore take no thought, saying, what shall we eat? Or, what shall we drink? Or, with what shall we be clothed? (For after all these things do the Gentiles seek :) for your heavenly Father knows that you have need of all these things. But seek first the kingdom of God, and his righteousness; and all these things shall be added unto you. (Matthew 6:31 -33)

We are urged there to have no anxiety regarding the things we eat or the clothes we wear. The reason for this is that as the children of God, we are not of the same pedigree as those without a relationship with Him. Our Father knows that we have material needs and has made it His responsibility to ensure that they are met as we pursue His Kingdom and righteousness.

But this I say, He that sows sparingly shall reap also sparingly; and he that sows bountifully shall reap also bountifully. Every man according as he purposes in his heart, so let him give; not grudgingly, or of necessity: for God loves a cheerful giver.

And God is able to make all grace abound toward you; so that you, always having all sufficiency in all things, may abound to every good work: (2 Corinthians 9:6-8)

Pursuing the Kingdom of God and His righteousness is to obey God's way of doing things and being in right standing with Him. Trusting God, generosity and kindness with material possessions results in God making more ability available to you. This ability enables you to have all sufficiency in all things. All means all! This means that you will have your needs met in every way.

The result of sufficiency in all things results in your ability to be abundant in good works. What are these good works? There are many good things that can be done with the material things that we have to the glory of God. There are many needs and purposes, all you need is to have a heart of godly compassion to see them and act upon them.

The phrase *"...abound to every good work"* is worthy of consideration. To *"abound"* is to overflow, to go beyond limits. In other words, God is able to make ability available to go beyond personal needs and be *abundant* (a variant of the root word *abound*) in good works. It is the will of God to supply you beyond that which meets your personal needs.

We ought to be content when we have sufficiency and work patiently and faithfully and our income will grow.

We will support this thought in the next part.

God will progressively grow material entrusted to you above your personal needs

His lord said unto him, well done, you good and faithful servant: you have been faithful over a few things, I will make you ruler over many things: enter you into the joy of thy lord. (Matthew 25:21)

He that is faithful in that which is least is faithful also in much: and he that is unjust in the least is unjust also in much. (Luke 16:10)

31

Wealth gotten by vanity shall be diminished: but he that gathers by labour shall increase. (Proverbs 13:11)

God rewards faithfulness by growing whatever you are faithful in. This is clear in the above text because *"...He that is faithful in that which is least is faithful also in much..."*

Faithfulness is doing what you have been assigned to do with diligence. God will reward your faithfulness by growing the material, abilities, talents, gifts and all that He has entrusted to you. *(Luke 19:17)*

Whoever is faithful in their work or other assignment committed to them will see it grow. This is the connection between godly success and material abundance. Work that is done diligently will grow and that growth will attract an increase in income, goods or other material.

The financial goal is not the focus, it is the bonus.

The goal is doing God's will to His specifications. Progressive growth in income associated with that work will be the outcome.

He that spared not his own Son, but delivered him up for us all, how shall he not with him also freely give us all things? (Romans 8:32)

God so loved the family of man that He gave up His Son, Jesus Christ to the cruel death of the cross to redeem them from death. Paul makes the point in the quoted verse through comparison. If God paid the price of the life of Jesus Christ on the cross on our behalf, how can He withhold anything else to bless us? Everything else is of lesser value, how can it be withheld from us?

This settles it for me. If God gave the greater in order to provide spiritual benefit, the lesser (material benefit) is a matter of course. Indeed, *"all things work together for the good of those who love God, to those who are the called according to His purpose" (Romans 8:28).* If Jesus was given up, everything else is at my disposal. I have the good and the bad, all working together for my advantage in Jesus Christ.

Unique callings and experiences

Surely, surely, I say unto you, When you were young, you clothed yourself, and walked where you wanted: but when you shall be old, you shall stretch forth your hands, and another shall clothe you, and carry you where you do not want. This he spoke, signifying by what death he should glorify God. And when he had spoken this, he said unto him, follow me. Then Peter, turning about, saw the disciple whom Jesus loved following; which also leaned on his breast at supper, and said, Lord, which is he that betrays you? Peter seeing him said to Jesus, Lord, and what shall this man do? Jesus said unto him, If I will that he remains till I come, what is that to you? You follow me. Then went this saying abroad among the brothers, that that disciple should not die: yet Jesus did not say unto him, He shall not die; but, If I will that he remain till I come, what is that to you? (John 21:18-23)

In conclusion, everything we have discussed in this chapter are the general terms of God's principles of success. However, it is important for every man to know that he has a unique way in which he will glorify God.

The Lord Jesus Christ's response to Peter's enquiry *"What will happen to John?"* was, *"What is that to you, you follow me."* This is the capstone. Everyone should pay attention to seek the fulfillment of the will of God with their life. To discover the will of God is to follow the Lord Jesus Christ.

Peter and John had unique ways in which they would glorify God with their lives. In the quoted text, the Lord Jesus shows Peter a future in which he would serve God and bring Him glory through suffering. This was Peter's unique portion and the Lord Jesus made sure that He let Him know it. Whoever follows the Lord Jesus wholeheartedly will undoubtedly receive a clear revelation of how they will glorify God with their life. When Peter sought to find a comparison between his experience and John's, the Lord Jesus Christ's response was clear. In today's language, the response could have been, *"Mind your own business, you follow me."* In other words, *"your experiences will be different; you focus on your portion and follow me."*

> *Then said Jesus unto his disciples, If any man will come after me, let him deny himself, and take up his cross, and follow me. (Matthew 16:24)*

Your unique portion with God is *your cross.* Your success, *making progress at achieving what God has intended* is taking up this cross and following the Lord Jesus Christ. You cannot take up your unique assignment in life if you do not deny yourself. You see how success is not empty ambition or the greed for material things? You cannot compare your achievements or possessions with the next person to measure your success. That is a wrong definition.

You have to compare yourself against God's standard for your life, His word, His cross. The true measuring line of a man's worth is the cross, that is why Jesus was stretched out on it.

What do I mean? You can only measure your success against what God intends for you, *your cross.* It is an assignment that God empowered you to achieve completely through the sacrifice of Jesus Christ on the cross. Your progress at achieving this is *success and your total well being (prosperity) depends on it.* This success by God's definition is the fundamental reason why you must *Overcome Procrastination.*

"THE TRUE MEASURING LINE OF A MAN'S WORTH IS THE CROSS"

4.

DESIRE & PRAYER

We cannot fully talk about delay if we do not talk about desires. There are things we want to accomplish in our lives and we are frustrated when we fail to do them. In the prior chapter, we went at length to show that success is the accomplishment of God's will (desire). We are going to show how your personal desires are connected to God's.

It is both very practical and spiritual to pay attention to your desires. I will prove this with two instances in the ministry of the Lord Jesus Christ.

Therefore I say unto you, what so-ever things you desire, when you pray, believe that you receive them, and you shall have them. (Mark 11:24)

Here, the Lord Jesus Christ refers to our desires as the starting point as he outlines the model of the prayer of faith. He does not say, *"In those things that the Father desires, when you pray..."* The reference point is *"our"* desires.

You and I have desires that the Lord respects and also desires to fulfill. The next line, *"when you pray"* takes us further in the process. It starts with our desires but certainly does not end there.

"What so-ever things you desire, when you pray," says the Lord Jesus Christ. This shows us that the first thing that must be done

with desire is prayer. Being the first thing that must be done about desire, it is a firm priority to overcome the procrastination of prayer.

"THE FIRST THING THAT MUST BE DONE WITH DESIRE IS PRAYER."

Prayer does not seem like action to a natural thinker. However, a spiritual thinker knows that you have begun to act when you begin to pray. The Lord Jesus Christ shows the process. If you have a desire, you must pray but prayer, being action, requires faith. *"...when you pray, believe..."* He says.

Having learnt *Mark 11:24*, you may desire to pray so that your hopes may be fulfilled. Nonetheless, you may experience a lack of prayer in your life. You may find yourself giving other activities the precedence. This results in prayer being relegated to *"a later, more appropriate time."* The main cause of procrastination regarding prayer is a lack of faith, which we will address in the next chapter.

In the meantime, there are a few wonderful facts about the desires of those who are born again. This is those who have responded faithfully to the message of chapter two, *"The Most Important, Most Urgent Message In The World."*

For he has made him to be sin for us, who knew no sin; that we might be made the righteousness of God in him. (2 Corinthians 5:21)

The fear of the wicked, it shall come upon him: but the desire of the righteous shall be granted. (Proverbs 10:24)

Those who are born again are *"the righteous."* Their faith in the salvation of Jesus Christ makes them so. I hope this is you. The writer of Proverbs declares a message that sets us apart from the world. Our desires are granted, they are never denied. When we pray, we are granted our requests. This is marvelous and ought to break the limits of delay from your mind to move your desires into manifestation. There is no doubt about it, your desires are granted.

Your new basic nature is righteousness. There is no innate desire for evil in you. If you were to desire evil, it is an exception and it has happened because you have decided not to be led by God's Spirit. Outside of this exception, those desires are most likely of God. Do not fear or ignore them.

> *Therefore if any man be in Christ, he is a new creature: old things are passed away; behold, all things are become new. (2 Corinthians 5:17)*

To be born again is not to merely follow the rites of a religion. We are not born again into a religion, we are totally transformed in life such that we are a new kind of creation, another species altogether. The habits and desires of a snake are different from those of the dove.

Their pursuits are distinctly different. Having received a new life, it comes with new and good desires which are in alignment with those of the God who has given spiritual birth to us.

"THE HABITS AND DESIRES OF THE SNAKE ARE DIFFERENT FROM THOSE OF THE DOVE."

If a righteous man were to desire something evil, that desire has not come from within him. That desire has been influenced from outside elements. This happens by paying attention to the messages and agendas that the devil continually tries to sell believers through this world system. We must bring our desires to the Lord in prayer. It is when we pray that we are able to prove the alignment of our desires with the will of God. The word of God is the will of God.

This is the encouragement that Paul gives in Romans 12:1-2.

> *I beg you therefore, brethren, by the mercies of God, that you present your bodies a living sacrifice, holy, acceptable unto*

God, which is your reasonable service. And be not conformed to this world: but be transformed by the renewing of your mind, that you may prove what is that good, and acceptable, and perfect, will of God. (Romans 12:1-2)

By bringing our desires in prayer, we are able to come to a place of aligning our thinking with that of the word of God. This is what the Lord Jesus Christ did in prayer at a crucial point in His life.

And he went a little further, and fell on his face, and prayed, saying, O my Father, if it be possible, let this cup pass from me: nevertheless not as I will, but as you will (Matthew 26:39)

He went away again the second time, and prayed, saying, O my Father, if this cup may not pass away from me, except I drink it, your will be done. (Matthew 26:42)

Let us take a look at the progression:

1. He brought His desire to the Father
    (let this cup pass from me)
2. He was open to the will of God
    (nevertheless not my will)
3. He progressed until He agreed with God's will
    (if this cup may not pass away from me, except I drink it, your will be done)

Everyone is called to do something by God. We will look at a few examples while holding true that God works the same way with all of His children. Jeremiah, John the Baptist and the Lord Jesus Christ were called for a specific purpose before their birth. God is no respecter of persons, so he will work in the same manner in your life.

Then Peter opened his mouth, and said, truly, I perceive that God is no respecter of persons: But in every nation he that fears him, and works righteousness, is accepted with him. (Acts 10:34-35)

Peter spoke to others in the book of Acts and argued that God was working with the rest of the Gentile world in the same way that He had worked with them as Jews. The same principle can be held true with how God works with us. If we can see examples of God working with man in the Bible, we can believe that He will use the same principles in dealing with us.

Before I formed you in the belly I knew you; and before you came out of the womb I sanctified you, and I ordained you a prophet unto the nations. (Jeremiah 1:5)

These were the words of God to Jeremiah from which we learn the principle of purposeful design. This is God's predetermined and specific assignments for individuals. For Jeremiah, the purpose for which he was designed was to be a prophet, and the sphere of his ministry was the nations or different cultural and tribal groups.

...the angel said unto him, Fear not, Zacharias: for your prayer is heard; and your wife Elisabeth shall bear you a son, and you shall call his name John. And you shall have joy and gladness; and many shall rejoice at his birth. For he shall be great in the sight of the Lord, and shall drink neither wine nor strong drink; and he shall be filled with the Holy Ghost, even from his mother's womb. And many of the children of Israel shall he turn to the Lord their God. And he shall go before him in the spirit and power of Elias, to turn the hearts of the fathers to the children, and the disobedient to the wisdom of the just; to make ready a people prepared for the Lord. (Luke 1:13-17)

John the Baptist was a forerunner of the Lord Jesus Christ. His conception and birth was announced to His father and mother beforehand. An angel appeared to Zacharias and announced the good news:

1. *They would have a son*
2. *His name would be "John"*
3. *He would bring joy to his parents and many*

4. *He would be great in God's sight*
5. *He would be filled with the Holy Spirit*
6. *He would turn the children of Israel to the Lord*
7. *His ministry would be similar to that of Elijah*

...the angel said unto her, Fear not, Mary: for you have found favour with God. And, behold, you shall conceive in thy womb, and bring forth a son, and shall call his name JESUS. He shall be great, and shall be called the Son of the Highest: and the Lord God shall give unto him the throne of his father David: And he shall reign over the house of Jacob for ever; and of his kingdom there shall be no end. (Luke 1:30-33)

For unto us a child is born, unto us a son is given: and the government shall be upon his shoulder: and his name shall be called Wonderful, Counsellor, The mighty God, The everlasting Father, The Prince of Peace. Of the increase of his government and peace there shall be no end, upon the throne of David, and upon his kingdom, to order it, and to establish it with judgment and with justice from henceforth even forever. The zeal of the LORD of hosts will perform this. (Isaiah 9: 6-7)

1. *They would have a son*
2. *His name would be Jesus*
3. *He would be great*
4. *He would reign over the House of Jacob forever*
5. *His Kingdom would not end*

In summary, from these three examples we learn:

1. *Predetermined purpose*
2. *Specific purpose*
3. *Place and space of operation*

The desires of your heart in life or what people have commonly called "their dreams" may *be the first clues or indicators of godly purpose and design*. This is a design in the same way that there was a clear purpose for Jeremiah, John the Baptist and the Lord Jesus Christ.

If you are born again, do not ignore your desires.

They may be the very first signal of what God has placed in your heart to achieve. There is a divine connection between *design, desire and destiny* which we must explore.

There are several ways through which God communicates His will.

Let us look at just three in order of priority:

The scriptures (the Bible)

Firstly, the principles of the word of God, the scriptures or the Bible are the will of God recorded through obedient servants of God for our guidance and example. There is nothing further that God will communicate in transgression of these principles. The scriptures are the primary source of God's will for our lives.

Promptings of the Holy Spirit and the desires of your heart

Secondly, if you are born again, you have the Holy Spirit in you. The Holy Spirit is the life of God in you. He is the one who activated eternal life in you when you believed. After you are born again, He is responsible for guiding you through your journey of maturity in Jesus Christ. He communicates the will of God in alignment to the word of God, directly to your heart.

The more you cooperate with the Holy Spirit, there will be a oneness of desire as He works in you. This is the wonderful dynamic recorded in the text below:

For it is God who works in you both to will and to do of his good pleasure (Philippians 2:13)

This working of God's will in your heart is the reason why we have said before *"If you are born again, do not ignore your desires."* Philippians 2:13 above shows how God works in you through the Holy Spirit to basically *"want what God wants."*

Personal prophecy from third parties

But the manifestation of the Spirit is given to every man to profit with all. For to one is given by the Spirit the word of wisdom; to another the word of knowledge by the same Spirit; To another the working of miracles; to another prophecy; to another discerning of spirits; to another divers kinds of tongues; to another the interpretation of tongues: (1 Corinthians 12:7 – 8, 10)

Lastly, through the revelation gifts of the Holy Spirit such as prophecy, wisdom and knowledge, God can use other believers to let you know His will. God uses this channel of direction as secondary to his communication directly to you. Being in you, the Holy Spirit would rather guide you through promptings to your heart and the influence of your desires. Nonetheless, the gifts of the Holy Spirit are a treasure in the church. You must earnestly desire to use them to encourage others. At the same time, there is nothing wrong with anticipating benefit from them as God uses others to encourage you.

You lust, and have not: you kill, and desire to have, and cannot obtain: you fight and war, yet you have not, because you ask not. (James 4:2)

The inability to ask God is proof that the request may be out of alignment with the word of God. The Word of God is the will of God. Prayer will clarify your desires' alignment with the will of God. Clarifying desires according to the will of God is important because it is also possible to have desires that are the product of worldly and external influences. We cannot say that these desires are the purpose of God. However, it suffices to say that the desires that you have are not to be ignored. There is nothing to lose. The word of God and prayer will clarify the matter and bring you closer to the achievement of Godly purpose.

"IF YOU ARE BORN AGAIN, DO NOT IGNORE YOUR DESIRES."

....I humbled my soul with fasting... (Psalm 35:13)

One sure way of discovering the will of God and overcoming selfish ambition or worldly influence is fasting and prayer. The writer of Psalms above gives us this wisdom. It has been taught that the soul is *"the seat of the intellect."* It is also the realm of decisions and emotions. The things we *"want"* or *"desire"* and how we *"feel"* is determined here. The soul, void of the influence and renewal of the word of God can lead you astray causing you to pursue things that God does not intend.

The discipline of fasting and prayer carries the power to *"humble"* this nature. Prayer, which is strengthened and intensified by fasting, carries the power to wrestle selfish and worldly desires to the ground. This allows the will of God to shine out so that you can do it.

Again, God actually works within us to begin to want and to do what pleases Him. This is what happens as you pray and fast. You allow God the opportunity to work out His will in your heart through the Holy Spirit. This is how your desires are proven. They must not be discarded; they must be tested to leave you holding onto the will of God.

I had a desire to speak and read in public way before I was born again. After I was born again, this desire resurfaced in a directed manner. I was sitting next to my pastor's son in church many years ago. I whispered into his ear, *"one day, I want to touch peoples' hearts like that with the word of God..."* as we listened to his dad preach. This was before I had even the slightest hint of a calling or ability to preach.

43

Over time, opportunities emerged for the gift and ability that already existed within me to be exhibited. I began to learn through experience what I had first known through desire.

In the chapter, *'Your Success Is God's Will'* we wrote:

"The one who does not care about achieving anything and doing it well has no need to mind the use of their time, nor the effectiveness of their efforts. This person can do whatsoever they want, when they want, and how they want. After all, they do not care about the outcome."

This is the reason we have spoken about desires. The mastery of procrastination, delay or postponement is only relevant for the one with a desirable objective to achieve.

"I BEGAN TO LEARN THROUGH EXPERIENCE WHAT I HAD FIRST KNOWN THROUGH DESIRE."

5.

HAVE FAITH IN GOD

Now faith is the substance of things hoped for, the evidence of things not seen. (Hebrews 11:1)

The captioned verse is interesting in that it is a direct Bible definition of what faith is. *"Now faith is the substance...,"* it says. The word translated *"substance"* above means *"a support."* In other words, and in continuation of our discourse in the last chapter:

Faith is a support for the desires you have.

"Desires" is a good replacement for *"things hoped for."* If you hope for something, it means that you want or desire it to happen. The realisation of desires is supported by faith. This implies that desires or hopes are held up by faith. If you remove faith, desires are castles in the sky, never coming to pass. If you want to think about it visually, the definition of faith tells us that desires fall flat and break into pieces without the support of the faith that holds them up.

We are talking about faith now because lack of faith is one of the reasons that important things are postponed. No action is taken regarding things that are regarded as important because the carrier of desire is bankrupt of the one essential currency that holds desires up until they become a tangible reality.

That word *"faith"* is a determinant regarding the fulfillment of desire. Without faith, you have an urge to do, become and have that never materializes. The absence of faith implies the presence of doubt and fear. It is one of the reasons that things are desired but are never done.

"DESIRES FALL FLAT AND BREAK INTO PIECES WITHOUT THE SUPPORT OF THE FAITH THAT HOLDS THEM UP"

Goals keep getting postponed to a later, *"more convenient"* time. This or they are utterly rejected as impossible, desirable but out of reach. You cannot act on your desires until you have faith because desires cannot stand upright without faith's support.

So how does faith support your desires or objectives? To answer this question, there is a need to give a further definition of faith. A leading teacher of the gospel of Jesus Christ in our day says about faith:

"It is the response of the human spirit to the word of God"

The word of God is the basis of faith. Faith is confidence that God is who He says He is and has the abilities that He says He has. Secondly, it is assurance that what He says about you and me is true.

"WITHOUT FAITH, YOU HAVE AN URGE TO DO, BECOME AND HAVE THAT NEVER MATERIALIZES."

Lastly, it is trust that His guidance on how to approach and deal with Him, people and things is dependable. All these things are outlined in the word of God. We have faith when we believe and rely on what the word of God says about these things.

So then faith comes by hearing, and hearing by the word of God. (Romans 10:17)

The words before the comma in the above text are worthy of isolated consideration. Faith in one thing or the other comes by hearing. In other words, what you pay attention to determines your confidence. If you pay attention to fear, worry and thoughts of failure, your confidence in their reality will grow. Fear and worry are mounting evidence that outcomes of disadvantage, failure, defeat and ultimately death will come to pass.

You cannot act on your desires when this is your disposition.

Procrastination becomes your trap because you cannot be prompt to act on what you believe will flop. You will postpone whatever you believe will have an unpleasant or failed outcome. On the other hand, you will hasten to do whatever you believe will give you an advantage and yield a successful outcome.

"FEAR AND WORRY ARE MOUNTING EVIDENCE THAT OUTCOMES OF DISADVANTAGE, FAILURE, DEFEAT AND ULTIMATELY DEATH WILL COME TO PASS"

The complete sentence *"So then faith comes by hearing, and hearing by the word of God"* completes the way to possess and grow in the God kind of faith. The phrase *"faith comes..."* implies that *"faith grows."* Faith will grow or mature according to your investment in the word of God. The more mature your faith, the better placed you are to place dependence on it. Immature faith may only be able to give mental and oral assent to the word of God.

Mature faith will be able to act on the basis of the word of God. *Romans 10:17* is one of the biblical foundations for the truth that:

The Word of God is the basis of faith.

There will be no growth in faith without the word of God. As you spend prayerful time in the word of God, the truth contained in it will convince you about:

1. *God*
2. *You and other people*
3. *Things*

These are the three dimensions regarding which you need faith in this life. The more your conscience is trained to trust God in relating to Him, yourself, other people and things, the more you will overcome delay in acting on what you desire to do. Let us see some of what the word of God says about these three dimensions of life. The three are presented according to faith's claim about each dimension.

"YOU CANNOT BE PROMPT TO ACT ON WHAT YOU BELIEVE WILL FLOP."

Faith claims the following things:

a. God's Personality and Ability are just as He claims in His Word *(He is who He says He is and He can do what He says He can do).*

This has the power to establish and grow your faith in God.

1. *He created the world (Genesis 1:1)*
2. *He is faithful (1 Corinthians 1:9)*
3. *He is all powerful (Hebrews 1:3)*
4. *His word is reliable (Isaiah 55:10-11)*
5. *He is a rewarder (Hebrews 11:6)*

b. Your Position and Provision are as God has outlined in His Word *(You are who God says you are and you have what He says you have).*

This carries the power to establish and grow your confidence in God about yourself.

1. *You have God's treasure within You (2 Corinthians 4:7)*
2. *You can cope in all situations through God's power (Philippians 4:13)*
3. *God has planned good things for You (Jeremiah 29:11)*
4. *You are not disadvantaged (Romans 8:28)*
5. *You are blessed (Ephesians 1:3)*

I am the vine, you are the branches: He that abides in me, and I in him, the same brings forth much fruit: for without me you can do nothing. (John 15:5)

For the believer, the common *"self-confidence"* mantra may be changed to *"God Confidence about me"* or rather,
"Confidence in God about me." This is because the human being is empty without God. The God factor cannot be excluded because without Him we can do nothing. It is God that gives us the ability to please Him and do anything that is of eternal value. This is why no Christian should carry a reference to *"self-made"* anything.

That said, you should have confidence that God has put abilities in you that are equal to the task. This is faith in what God has placed in you. Without this confidence, you anticipate failure and are unwilling to get down to action and get things done promptly.

Procrastination is overcome when you arise in this confidence. You are able by God's grace!

c. God's guidance on how to approach and deal with Him, people and things is reliable.

1. *Pray in faith and you will receive (Mark 11:24)*
2. *Desires are supported by faith (Hebrews 11:1)*

3. *God cannot be pleased without faith (Hebrews 11:6)*
4. *Give and you will receive (Luke 6:38)*
5. *It is better to give than to receive (Acts 20:35)*

Your view of God, yourself, others and things is a determinant of your promptness to action. This view is really your faith in God regarding these things. This faith is determined by your hearing and meditating in the word of God. The more you receive the word, the greater your faith. Great faith produces great promptness to act.

But without faith it is impossible to please him: for he that comes to God must believe that he is, and that he is a rewarder of them that diligently seek him. (Hebrews 11:6)

If it is impossible for God to receive pleasure when you do not have faith, neither can you. Doubt and fear, which results in unfulfilled desire may be a major cause of frustration and unhappiness amongst believers. The opposite of pleasure is sorrow, grief, dissatisfaction, unhappiness and discontent. When you desire and do not have, you become unhappy because the longings of your inner man are unfulfilled. You may have comfort and possessions on the outside, but if the desire of the inner man is unfulfilled, you cannot know lasting peace and joy.

Hope deferred makes the heart sick: but when the desire comes, it is a tree of life (Proverbs 13:12)

Your desires are your hopes. When they are delayed in fulfillment, you lack peace and cannot secure lasting joy and happiness. As long as the desires of the real you *(inner man, spirit)* are not accomplished, it does not matter what is at the disposal of the costume *(body)* on the outside. There will be no joy and peace.

When I have a book to finish, a message to preach or an important assignment to complete, I am uneasy until I do it. I become a liability to those who want to pull me into other activities to relax or *"have a good time."* I cannot happily have a good time until I have completed

50

the assignments that I believe God has given to me. This is expressed by the Lord Jesus Christ when He is resigned from food to dedicate Himself to preach the Kingdom of God. He explains it to His disciples after they attempt to convince Him to eat some food:

> ....*My meat is to do the will of him that sent me, and to finish his work (John 4:34)*

The above means that the Lord Jesus Christ found that His fulfillment and satisfaction came from completing the assignments committed to Him. The alternative is clearly internal dissatisfaction which may manifest outwardly as frustration, sorrow and irritability.

> *Up to this point you have asked nothing in my name: ask, and you shall receive, that your joy may be full. (John 16:24)*

Joy and peace comes from the fulfillment of desire.

Desire cannot be fulfilled without prayer *(asking God)*. Prayer cannot be successful without faith.

Making a request requires one of two things, ignorance or boldness. You can approach God out of presumption and get ashamed when you do not receive. On the other hand, you can approach with boldness, knowing the terms of the relationship and the grounds upon which you are guaranteed to receive. This boldness is a characteristic of faith.

In conclusion, the definition of faith again as rendered in *Hebrews 11:1* is *"...the substance/assurance of things hoped for, the evidence of things not seen."* Another way of interpreting that is to say *"faith is the guarantee of the future."* Hope is for the future but faith is what guarantees that future NOW. This is clear, because if faith is the *"assurance of things hope for"* then it is required now, before the future arrives.

The desire or hope for the future must be taken to the word of God and prayer where it will be exposed as lust or legitimate desire based on faith. When faith is grasped, it is prompt to act. Action is the only evidence of mature faith. When faith is mature, it acts. Do you know people who only talk and pray a lot about their desires and goals but they never do anything about them? Maybe you are one of them. I was one of them once.

And when you pray, you shall not be as the hypocrites are: for they love to pray standing in the synagogues and in the corners of the streets, that they may be seen of men. Surely I say unto you, they have their reward. (Matthew 6:5)

Now I know that speech may only be the evidence of one of two things, beliefs or hypocrisy. Beliefs are not faith. They are part of the lifecycle of grasping faith, but they are not faith. Beliefs alone don't change lives, faith does. Belief can talk, faith can act. Hypocrisy or pretense is when someone speaks or behaves in a way that they would like to be perceived. This is not who they really are, however, they talk and act the part to be seen.

"BELIEFS ALONE DON'T CHANGE LIVES, FAITH DOES. BELIEF CAN TALK, FAITH CAN ACT."

Therefore, talking is not enough, whether it is to others or to God in prayer. It may be the evidence of beliefs; this is good but not good enough. Worse, talking may be the evidence of hypocrisy, which is a thing that God hates. The reward of hypocrisy is a false reputation for doing well. This is not what you want.

Be real, have faith and act. You will receive the reward of fulfilled desire.

"WHEN FAITH IS GRASPED, IT IS PROMPT TO ACT."

6.

ACT NOW & GROW YOUR ABILITIES

One of the factors that may be responsible for the postponing of action may be the intimidation associated with taking on a task. When you are small in your own eyes, most opposition looks like a giant and barriers look like mountains.

Most of us are small in our own eyes when we take on a new thing. We require the encouragement of the word of God to overcome. Most servants of God were intimidated by the task when God called them.

Gideon said "....my family is the poorest in Manasseh, and I am the least in my father's house." (Judges 6:15)

Moses said "I am not eloquent....I am slow of speech, and of slow tongue."(Exodus 4:10)

Jeremiah said "..... I do not know how to speak; for I am a child" (Jeremiah 1:6)

Solomon said "I do not know how to go out or come in" (1 Kings 3:7)

Paul had to encourage Timothy, ".....Let no man despise thy youth....." (1 Timothy 4:12) and again:

"....God has not given us a spirit of fear...." (2 Timothy 1:7)

Do not be intimidated by your perception of inability.

Ability grows through use. Scale, growth and power come through faithfulness at doing what you can *now*, however small. In *Hebrews 5:14* below, the context refers to the development of believers to maturity in their faith.

"ABILITY GROWS THROUGH USE."

But strong meat belongs to them that are of full age, even those who by reason of use have their senses exercised to discern both good and evil. (Hebrew 5:14)

The writer notes that the believers he is addressing ought to have developed and become teachers at that stage rather than still wait to be taught by others. In making his point, the writer reveals that advanced spiritual food, that is, the advanced principles of the word of God are appropriate for the mature.

According to the last part of the verse, *"the mature"* or *"those that are of full age"* are those who have grown by exercising or using their spiritual senses. To exercise or use the spiritual senses refers to the application of the word of God in a believer's life. It is use or application that results in growth. Let us look at another text that echoes this very thing.

For the kingdom of heaven is as a man travelling into a far country, who called his own servants, and delivered unto them his goods. And unto one he gave five talents, to another two, and to another one; to every man according to his several ability; and straight away took his journey. Then he that had received the five talents went and traded with the same, and made them other five talents. And likewise he that had received two, he also gained other two. But he that had received one went and dug in the earth, and hid his lord's money. After a long time, the lord of those servants returned, and reckoned with them. And so he that had received five talents came and brought other five talents, saying, Lord, you delivered unto me five talents: behold, I have gained beside them five talents more. His lord said unto him, well done, you good and faithful servant: you have been faithful over a few things, I will make you ruler over many things: enter you into the joy of your lord. He also that had received two talents came and said, Lord, you delivered unto me two talents: behold, I have gained two other talents beside them. His lord said unto him, well done, good and faithful servant; you have been faithful over a few things, I will make you ruler over many things: enter you into the joy of your lord. Then he which had received the one talent came and said, Lord, I knew you that you are a hard man, reaping where you have not sown, and gathering where you have not strawed: And I was afraid, and went and hid your talent in the earth: look, here is what belongs to you. His lord answered and said unto him, you wicked and slothful servant, you knew that I reap where I sowed not, and gather where I have not strawed: you ought therefore to have put my money to the exchangers, and then at my coming I should have received mine own with interest. Take therefore the talent from him, and give it unto him who has ten talents. For unto every one that has shall be given, and he shall have abundance: but from him that has not shall be taken away even that which he has. And cast the unprofitable servant into outer darkness: there shall be weeping and gnashing of teeth. (Matthew 25:14-30)

In the same way that the travelling man gave his money to his servants' care and travelled, God has committed *His goods* through gifts and talents to each and every person in this world. This is no matter how void of giftedness or opportunity you think you are. Regardless of how small you seem to yourself, there is an investment that God has put within you. There is latent power or potential to be fruitful that you possess. It is God's investment in every human being. This is the premise of this text in the book of Genesis:

So God created man in his own image, in the image of God created he him; male and female created he them. And God blessed them, and God said unto them, Be fruitful, and multiply, and replenish the earth, and subdue it: and have dominion over the fish of the sea, and over the fowl of the air, and over every living thing that moves upon the earth. (Genesis 1:27-28)

Fruitfulness and multiplication flows from planted seed. There can be no fruit if there is no seed. This means that God has a seed of productivity and growth in each and every person that comes to the face of this earth. It is God's gift to humanity. If this was not true, the command to be fruitful and multiply would be misplaced. *"Be fruitful and multiply"* is an appropriate command where seed has been planted.

You would not expect fruit from a piece of ground in which you have not planted seed; likewise God would not expect fruit from humanity he has not invested potential in. In addition, you cannot multiply nothing. It is a mathematical fundamental that zero multiplied by a million is still zero. Everyone carries the capacity to grow their abilities and the things committed to their trust.

"BE FRUITFUL AND MULTIPLY IS AN APPROPRIATE COMMAND WHERE SEED HAS BEEN PLANTED"

So it is settled that all of humanity carries potential that they are supposed to grow. This potential or resources are committed according to each one's *capability*. Everyone has differing capability. This capability is the ability or capacity to handle responsibility or assignment. This initial capability is God given and by divine sovereignty. So is God unfair, dealing more capacity to one than another? No, he is all fair and just and deals to all according to His will and unique purposes. Take a look at how God dealt between Jacob and Esau and how Paul explains that God calls his people to a purpose in advance.

Though they were not yet born and had done nothing either good or bad—in order that God's purpose of election might continue, not because of works but because of him who calls—she was told, "The older will serve the younger." As it is written, "Jacob I loved, but Esau I hated." What shall we say then? Is there injustice on God's part? By no means! For he says to Moses, "I will have mercy on whom I have mercy, and I will have compassion on whom I have compassion." So then it depends not on human will or exertion, but on God, who has mercy. (Romans 9:11-16) (ESV)

This is the same principle in the parable, where the Lord Jesus taught that:

....unto one he gave five talents, to another two, and to another one; to every man according to his several ability... (Matthew 25:15)

Each servant received *something*. None was left without responsibility. The only thing that differed was the amount entrusted to them. By working with his servants, the master was familiar with their abilities and so he did not give them responsibility beyond them.

After hearing the full story of how the master dealt with his servants, you can tell his justice. You find that regardless of how much a servant started with, each carried the opportunity to grow their endowment doubly through diligence and faithfulness.

Then he that had received the five talents went and traded with the same, and made them other five talents. And likewise he that had received two, he also gained other two. But he that had received one went and dug in the earth, and hid his lord's money (Matthew 25v16-18)

There was growth of responsibility for two of the servants but one of them remained where they were. The difference maker, regardless of how much they started with was *what they did with what they had.* By the time the season was over, they were no longer where they started. Their activities made the difference. The five and two talent servants understood the principle of fruitfulness and multiplication tied to every ability and possession we have. There is a God ordained requirement to grow and multiply whatever is placed under the authority of your hand. They *traded with* or *used* what they had and it resulted in multiplication. On the other hand, the one talent servant did nothing meaningful with the money. All he had when the season ended was the very thing he started with. Nothing was added to it because there was no use.

> ## "THERE IS A GOD ORDAINED
> ## REQUIREMENT TO GROW
> ## AND MULTIPLY WHATEVER
> ## IS PLACED UNDER THE
> ## AUTHORITY OF YOUR HAND"

Well done, good and faithful servant; you have been faithful over a few things, I will make you ruler over many things: enter you into the joy of your lord. (Matthew 25v21, 23)

The five and two talent servants received praise from their Lord and the promise that their responsibilities would grow. Along with the growth in their portfolio, they also entered *into the joy of their Lord.* This is the place of satisfaction, celebration and honour that comes with fulfilling their master's assignment. Faithfulness is doing what you have been assigned to do with diligence. God will reward your faithfulness by growing your abilities and responsibilities.

His lord answered and said unto him, you wicked and slothful servant, you knew that I reap where I sowed not, and gather where I have not strawed: you ought therefore to have put my money to the exchangers, and then at my coming I should have received mine own with interest. Take therefore the talent from him, and give it unto him who has ten talents. For unto every one that has shall be given, and he shall have abundance: but from him that has not shall be taken away even that which he has. And cast the unprofitable servant into outer darkness: there shall be weeping and gnashing of teeth (Matthew 25:26-30)

The one talent servant received a stinging rebuke from his master because of his inactivity and lack of productivity. He was called *wicked, lazy and unprofitable.* These were strong words but fitting. His wickedness was in his defiance of his master's requirement for growth. His laziness was in doing nothing. His unprofitability was in failing to grow what he was given. The five and two talent servants were rewarded with multiplication for their faithfulness. On the other hand, the one talent servant lost even that which he had hid in the earth to the servant who had demonstrated an ability to handle more. In other words, what was taken away from him was added to another.

An interesting thing here is that the talents were committed to the servants *according to their ability* to begin with. We have already taught above that *"ability grows through use."* When the two and five talent servants traded, their ability grew. When their ability grew, their master was ready to give them more. He took away from one and committed it to the one who had grown his ability the most. I can be almost sure that when the next round would come around, the two talent servant would have been promoted to perhaps a five talent servant!

Waiting does not help the matter. It will only work frustration and make you weaker. Gain power by doing. Muscles grow through use. The thought, *"I will wait till I can lift that one"* is foolishness and *"I will lift this one until I can lift that one"* is wisdom.

"GAIN POWER BY DOING. MUSCLES GROW THROUGH USE"

Your desire and conviction to do something through faith is God's calling and assignment. Act now and do it with faithfulness and your abilities will grow.

Who goes to war any time at his own charge? ... (1 Corinthians 9:7)

God does not call you ill equipped. No soldier is conscripted to war with his own resources. He does not buy his own uniform, armour or food. All is provided by the custodians of the mission he has been called to serve. Likewise, your abilities may be in potential but they are there. God would not call you without them.

This would be a call to failure that God certainly does not sponsor.

Whatsoever your hand finds to do, do it with your might; for there is no work, nor device, nor knowledge, nor wisdom, in the grave, where you are headed (Ecclesiastes 9:10)

With that background, it is important to note that every desire, idea, talent, gift, dream, vision, opportunity or goal has a date of discovery and a date of expiry. The word of God teaches us what to do at the point of discovery, with those things that we *"find."* To find is to discover. The prescription when you discover a desire, a gift, a dream or an opportunity is to take immediate action. There is no time to wait or waste. The date and time of action is the date and time of discovery.

All the men we outlined earlier had to overcome their fears and inhibitions. This is why we had to deal with faith prior to this chapter. Faith has overcome doubt and fear. Faith has confidence in God as well as in that which God has provided.

"EVERY DESIRE, IDEA, TALENT, GIFT, DREAM, VISION, OPPORTUNITY OR GOAL HAS A DATE OF DISCOVERY AND A DATE OF EXPIRY"

And Samuel said unto Jesse, Are these all your children? And he said, There remains yet the youngest, and, behold, he keeps the sheep. And Samuel said unto Jesse, Send and fetch him: for we will not sit down till he comes here. (1 Samuel 16:11)

And Eliab his eldest brother heard when he spoke unto the men; and Eliab's anger was ignited against David, and he said, why did you come down here? And with whom have you left those few sheep in the wilderness? I know your pride, and the naughtiness of your heart; for you have come down that you may see the battle. (1 Samuel 17:28)

And David said unto Saul, your servant kept his father's sheep, and there came a lion, and a bear, and took a lamb out of the flock: I went after him and struck him and delivered it out of his mouth. And if he arose against me, I caught him by his beard and struck him and killed him. Your servant has struck down both lions and bears, and this uncircumcised Philistine shall be like one of them, for he has defied the armies of the living God. (1Samuel 17:34-36)

Therefore David ran, and stood upon the Philistine, and took his sword, and drew it out of the sheath thereof, and slew him, and cut off his head therewith. And when the Philistines saw their champion was dead, they fled. (1 Samuel 17:51)

When Samuel came to anoint or separate one of Jesse's sons to be king, David was not at home. David was in the field with his father's sheep. He seems not to have been considered as a contender for the choice because the lineup was placed before Samuel in his absence. It was only after the prophet Samuel could not find God's choice amongst the big boys that he enquired whether everyone was there. Sure enough, there was one who was not present, the youngest, David. This first part of David's story culminated in him, the youngest being anointed king.

The evidence of despise is seen later when David visits the battlefront having been sent with food for his brothers. Eliab, the eldest rebukes him for coming to the battle, deferring him and denigrating him to the menial with the words *"Why did you come down here? And with whom have you left those few sheep in the wilderness?" (1 Samuel 17:28).* This is the common attitude of the world toward potential.

There are only a few who can recognize and give potential a chance. Most can only appreciate a thing when it has fully manifested. Regardless of his brother's seeming ridicule, it did not take long for a common lunch trip to become an appointment with destiny as David gets an audience with the king.

In a nation full of men, young and old, what set David apart from the rest? What gave him the opportunity to speak with the great? Well, firstly, it was the fact that God had chosen him for it, anointing him to set him apart from the common. This distinction working in his life made David behave differently from the rest. When the rest of the nation cowered in fear, David was different. Instead, he observed the sight of a whole nation terrified of an ungodly opponent and refused to accept it. Where others spoke of their terror and hopelessness, he spoke a different language of victory. David's distinct response to the challenge gave him his first audience with the king. Likewise, your language of faith in the face of tough situations will draw God's attention.

> *And when the words were heard which David spoke, they rehearsed them before Saul: and he sent for him. And David said to Saul, Let no man's heart fail because of him; your servant will go and fight with this Philistine. And Saul said to David, you are not able to go against this Philistine to fight with him: for you are but a youth, and he is a man of war from his youth. (1 Samuel 17:31-33)*

"DAVID'S DISTINCT RESPONSE TO THE CHALLENGE GAVE HIM HIS FIRST AUDIENCE WITH THE KING"

Courageous enough to come before the king and ask for the opportunity to face a national problem, David is confronted by the challenge of natural assessment. The king says to David, *"...you are not able to go against this Philistine to fight with him: for you are only a youth, and he is a man of war from his youth."* Coming from the king, these words should have decimated his resolve to take this challenge head on but it did not. This was the story of his life. He was left out of the line-up to be anointed king because he was only the youngest and they probably thought, *"it cannot be him..."* When he began to enquire regarding the threats that he heard Goliath make, his own brother was angry with him and referred him back to his normal life.

Young David was not deterred; it was as though he had heard the words of the apostle Paul:

Let no man despise your youth; but be an example of the believers, in word, in conversation, in charity, in spirit, in faith, in purity. (1 Timothy 4:12)

These things speak, and exhort, and rebuke with all authority. Let no man despise you. (Titus 2:15)

The Holy Spirit led Paul to speak about it because it is a recognised problem. Youth and inexperience will be despised but it is the duty of the despised not to allow it to prosper. You are supposed to keep your faith and resolve to do what you are called to do in the face of the actions and utterances of those who cannot discern the calling of greatness in your life.

Denigrating looks, words and votes of no confidence may issue from the great and the small. These are the actions of the carnal, those who refuse to consider every person by the revelation of the Holy Spirit preferring to judge with their natural eyes. Facing this opposition, the way to victory is to refuse to retreat and consult the higher opinion of the God who called you.

David responded to the king with reference to his track record with God in private. It was a track record of action! God was about to change David's life in a day but God had prepared him for it for

63

years. The young boy recounted to the king, *"there came a lion, and a bear, and took a lamb out of the flock: I went after him and struck him and delivered it out of his mouth. And if he arose against me, I caught him by his beard and struck him and killed him."*

This was testimony that his time in the pastures was not a time of idleness or leisure. It was a time of action. The arena of his battles was smaller and his challenges, though fierce were not as great as the giant that intimidated a whole nation. David's abilities grew through use and action, including the ability to see a victory where others were convinced of defeat. David's is an inspiring story of *"a little one, becoming like an army"* It happened because he was obedient to the principle, *"act now and grow your abilities."*

It is not easy for man to give you a chance at something big. People are usually comfortable when you are doing the common, preferring to keep you where you have always been. Uncommon moves are uncomfortable to the common man. When you are in this place, your opportunity can only come from God.

You will gain traction in life through action and not through mere speech. Trying to sell yourself to others as able is a waste of time. Perform the doing of a thing and the proof is clear. Getting a platform for greatness with those who despise you may be a challenge but when God has prepared you for a large scale public problem, the time will come when your spot on the team cannot be denied. When the position is ordained for you, the coach's decision to exclude you will be a choice to lose the match.

> ## "WHEN THE POSITION IS ORDAINED FOR YOU, THE COACH'S DECISION TO EXCLUDE YOU WILL BE A CHOICE TO LOSE THE MATCH."

The time will come when the problem will be so large and they will all be afraid. A gigantic problem is intimidating to anyone who does not carry the anointing or the power to overcome it. On the other hand, to the one who is empowered by God to conquer a problem, it is like bread. When you are chosen, your time will certainly come to step up and do something about it.

On that day, you will not need to convince anyone that you are able; the giant's head in your hands will be the solid proof of your abilities.

And as soon as David returned from the striking down of the Philistine, Abner took him, and brought him before Saul with the head of the Philistine in his hand. (1 Samuel 17:57)

Results are hard to despise. With the proof of victory in his hand, David was brought before the king. The king wanted to know more about him. The difference maker in David's life was the action he took, not the good thoughts he had about his future. It was when he garnered enough courage and faith to do what he had never done before that he moved from obscurity to prominence. Let us close these thoughts with a caption from the book of Ecclesiastes:

He who observes the wind will not sow, and he who regards the clouds will not reap. As you do not know the way the spirit comes to the bones in the womb of a woman with child, so you do not know the work of God who makes everything. In the morning sow your seed, and at evening withhold not your hand, for you do not know which will prosper, this or that, or whether both alike will be good. (Ecclesiastes 11:4-6)

You cannot depend on the outward state of things to determine when it is the right time to act. That is not the right source of information. In fact, the wisdom that Solomon gave in the above text signifies that circumstances will rarely cooperate with a productive course of action. There will always be reasons why now is not the right time to act.

Faith is not determined by circumstance but circumstances are determined by faith. The contrary is a choice to be a slave to life. Faith is concerned by the word of God. If the word of God says it, faith is determined to act with disregard to prevailing conditions.

We are called to obey the word, our calling, our understanding of God's purpose for our lives. We do not know how God works it all out but our only duty is to act in alignment with the word and God's revealed will for our lives. Act now, and grow your abilities.

**"CIRCUMSTANCES WILL
RARELY COOPERATE WITH
A PRODUCTIVE COURSE OF
ACTION."**

7.

PLAN

We have already dealt with the delays that we suffer because we have no confidence in our abilities. Now we want to deal with procrastination because of the absence of clear goals. The job may look so big that we do not know where to start and put it off to as far down the lane as possible.

There is the tendency to mill around doing non- essential and lower priority tasks while avoiding the main and highest priority task on the list. Why? This is because we tend to avoid and postpone our pain. This is natural. We avoid pain just like a river takes the path of least resistance and winds its way around, avoiding the harder terrain.

I said *"this is natural,"* I did not say, *"It is acceptable."* This is a natural disposition which must be overcome by spiritual people.

Picture a neat, green football pitch and twenty-two players sprawled over it. There is also a twenty-third man in black on pitch with a sparkling silver whistle hung round his neck. Where is the ball? Oh, there it is. All set? Not so fast! You check left and right and there are no goal posts. Twenty two men chasing a ball for ninety minutes with no goal posts on either side could make good comedy but that is all. God does not reward comics. Everything else will be in position except the means by which the outcome of the whole game is determined. A lack of goal setting may be one of the basic causes of a lack of prompt action.

"TWENTY TWO MEN CHASING A BALL FOR NINETY MINUTES WITH NO GOAL POSTS COULD MAKE GOOD COMEDY BUT THAT IS ALL. GOD DOES NOT REWARD COMICS."

So what is a goal? A goal is a broad statement of what will be achieved. An example of a goal may be given as:

Develop a framework to overcome the bad habit of procrastination.

When there are no goal posts on the field:

1. *The direction of play cannot be determined*
2. *Confusion abounds*
3. *Progress cannot be measured*
4. *Brilliance or mediocrity cannot be identified*
5. *The incentive for excellence and discipline is missing*

The progress of the entire game is measured and determined by the very positioning of those goal posts. It has been said by some thought leaders, *"you cannot manage what you cannot measure."*

If you cannot measure a shot on or off target, you cannot manage good or bad striking performance.

Basically, you trudge along in an effort whose value addition to your life you cannot measure. Other terms related to the matter of goals are:

1. Objectives
This is a specific, measurable outcome to which time is associated.
2. Activities and Tasks
This is work performed toward an outlined objective. Tasks detail the work assigned to individuals according to defined timelines.

These may be considered granular or detailed aspects of goals. For the sake of simplicity I will use the terms *"goals," "objectives,"* and *"activities," "tasks"* interchangeably.

In that light, good goals must identify:

1. *What must be done*
2. *Who must do it*
3. *The target date by which it must be done*

If you exclude the aspect of time, you have aimed well at what must be done but you have ignored how long the endeavour should take. In this situation, you can have a good goal that takes forever to accomplish. You cannot achieve what you do not take aim at. You usually fit your efforts within the time that is made available to you such that a 5 day job that is given a 14 day deadline may actually take 15 days to deliver. A target date must be associated with a goal or the objectives that support it; otherwise we may deliver a good but irrelevant outcome. Time changes the context of things, retiring the relevance of an objective.

What would you do if you had the following task?

Gathering together trillions of litres of water. In addition, providing quadrillions of tons of gigantic land mass *(million, billion, trillion...quadrillion)* to stand alongside that water.

You think your job is done? Not at all. Now you have the formidable task of suspending that massive, colossal, gigantic mass of land and water in mid air, hanging on nothing but....nothing.

As though that were not enough, you had to make a gigantic ball of fire and also suspend that in mid air, again on nothing. You had to be careful that it is just the right distance away from the land and water mass.

The ball of fire has to be far enough away not to destroy the land and boil the water but close enough to keep everything from freezing over.

Now you decide to make sure that there is a relationship between the land and water mass and the ball of fire. You want the land and water mass to spin around the ball of fire at an average speed of about 29.8km per second or 107,000km per hour[1] while spinning at its own centre....without spilling any of the water or destroying the things on the land mass.

To top it all off, you had to crown the whole project by making a living, thinking miraculous creation that is able to balance itself on two feet walking upright. You make that creature and keep him in balance while the land and water mass is spinning.

What an interesting way to look at creation! This is the picture: God had a massive task and the record shows us that God used a method to manage it. We can learn wisdom from the pattern because the scriptures teach us that we are to imitate our heavenly Father as his beloved children:

Therefore, be imitators of God as well-beloved children (Ephesians 5:1)

The creation process is a miracle beyond mere mental comprehension. The bible narrates it and the one who is born again believes it.

So what is the pattern we see from creation? It has been postulated by many speakers and writers that the way to overcome the intimidation of a massive project is to break it down into smaller portions.

Breaking down a task divides the work into objectives that can be engaged and accomplished in manageable bite sizes little by little. It is a valid piece of advice and I will lend you its biblical basis.

From *Genesis Chapter 1 verse 1 to 31*, God divided the massive creation project into six days of work. Faith has goals; it plans and breaks down an intimidating task into little pieces that it is able to chew little by little.

Now faith is the substance of things hoped for, the evidence of things not seen. (Hebrews 11:1)

---

1   http://en.wikipedia.org/wiki/Earth - Orbit

Faith is the assurance of *"things."* Things may be interpreted as goals and objectives. The desires of our faith must not be hazy or indefinite. You must be able to crystallize your desires into clear goals that you desire to come to pass. One writer has said, *"the clearer your goals, the greater your faith."* On the other hand, where there are no goals, anything goes.

The broad, overall target and reason for your efforts is the goal. The smaller tasks that you need to do in order to accomplish your goal are the objectives. There are many objectives for one goal. Look at it this way, with the football pitch example:

1. The Goal: *Place the ball past the goal keeper, into the net.*
2. The Objectives: *The many ball passes from player to player that build up to the scoring of the goal, each timed to perfection.*

"WHERE THERE ARE NO GOALS, ANYTHING GOES"

The six days of creation were focused on fulfilling a clear goal, which may be *"To bring order where there was chaos."* The objectives were the many tasks that went into achieving the goal over six days. In the same way, every goal you have will usually be accomplished through several objectives that support it.

No-one can convince me that the goals accomplished on each day were accidental, adhoc or by chance. God is more precise than that. The Lord Jesus said of Him,

"The very hairs of your head are all numbered (by Him)" and *"not one (of the birds) falls from the sky without His knowledge"* (Matthew 10:29-30). He is *"hair strand"* precise if you like, and that is an understatement.

For the goals that you want to achieve in a year for example, there must be several objectives that build up to their achievement every day. This is what God did and we are fool hardy if we ignore His blueprint for getting things done.

To discover worthy goals, you need to ask yourself the accomplishments that will earn you a reward. Why a reward? This is because your goals must be worthwhile; otherwise you will not pay the price to accomplish them. Every worthy goal will place a demand on you for discipline. The reward is your incentive to harness your propensities for comfort and ease. The seventh day of rest was the reward for six days of creation.

Let us take a look at God's creation schedule:

Day 1

And God said, Let there be light: and there was light. And God saw the light, that it was good: and God divided the light from the darkness. And God called the light Day, and the darkness he called Night. And the evening and the morning were the first day. (Genesis 1:3-5)

1. *Light*
2. *Separation of Light from Darkness*
3. *Naming of Light, Day and Darkness, Night*

Day 2

And God said, Let there be a firmament in the midst of the waters, and let it divide the waters from the waters. And God made the firmament, and divided the waters which were under the firmament from the waters which were above the firmament: and it was so. And God called the firmament Heaven. And the evening and the morning were the second day. (Genesis 1:6-8)

1. *Heaven*
2. *Separation of water*

Day 3

And God said, Let the waters under the heaven be gathered together unto one place, and let the dry land appear: and it was so. And God called the dry land Earth; and the gathering together of the waters called he Seas: and God saw that it was good. And God said, Let the earth bring forth grass, the herb yielding seed, and the fruit tree yielding fruit after his kind, whose seed is in itself, upon the earth: and it was so. And the earth brought forth grass, and herb yielding seed after his kind, and the tree yielding fruit, whose seed was in itself, after his kind: and God saw that it was good. And the evening and the morning were the third day. (Genesis 1:9-13)

1. *Gathering of the water into one place*
2. *Creation of dry land*
3. *Naming of the dry land as Earth*
4. *Naming of the gathered water as Seas*
5. *Creation of vegetation with seed in it*
6. *Creation of the tree that bears fruit with seed in it*

Day 4

And God said, Let there be lights in the firmament of the heaven to divide the day from the night; and let them be for signs, and for seasons, and for days, and years: And let them be for lights in the firmament of the heaven to give light upon the earth: and it was so. And God made two great lights; the greater light to rule the day, and the lesser light to rule the night: he made the stars also. And God set them in the firmament of the heaven to give light upon the earth, And to rule over the day and over the night, and to divide the light from the darkness: and God saw that it was good. And the evening and the morning were the fourth day. (Genesis 1:14-19)

1. *Creation of a greater light, the Sun*
2. *Creation of a lesser light, the Moon*

3. *Greater light by design is assigned to rule the day*
4. *Lesser light by design is assigned to rule the night*
5. *Creation of Time, Signs and Seasons*
6. *Separation of Day from Night*
7. *The creation of the Stars*

Day 5

And God said, Let the waters bring forth abundantly the moving creature that hath life, and fowl that may fly above the earth in the open firmament of heaven. And God created great whales, and every living creature that moveth, which the waters brought forth abundantly, after their kind, and every winged fowl after his kind: and God saw that it was good. And God blessed them, saying, Be fruitful, and multiply, and fill the waters in the seas, and let fowl multiply in the earth. And the evening and the morning were the fifth day. (Genesis 1:20-23)

1. *The creation of Sea life*
2. *The creation of Bird life*
3. *Fruitfulness and multiplication of Sea and Bird life*

Day 6

And God said, Let the earth bring forth the living creature after his kind, cattle, and creeping thing, and beast of the earth after his kind: and it was so. And God made the beast of the earth after his kind, and cattle after their kind, and every thing that creepeth upon the earth after his kind: and God saw that it was good. And God said, Let us make man in our image, after our likeness: and let them have dominion over the fish of the sea, and over the fowl of the air, and over the cattle, and over all the earth, and over every creeping thing that creepeth upon the earth. So God created man in his own image, in the image of God created he him; male and female created he them. And God blessed them, and God said unto them, Be fruitful, and multiply, and replenish the earth, and subdue it: and have dominion over the fish of the sea, and over the fowl of the air, and over every living thing that moveth upon the earth. And God said, Behold, I have given you every herb bearing seed, which is upon the face of all the earth, and every tree, in the which is the fruit of a tree yielding seed; to you it shall be for meat. And to every beast of the earth, and to every fowl of the air, and to every thing that creepeth upon the earth, wherein there is life, I have given every green herb for meat: and it was so. And God saw every thing that he had made, and, behold, it was very good. And the evening and the morning were the sixth day. (Genesis 1:24-31)

1. *The creation of Animal life*
2. *Creation of Reptile, Insect and other creature life*
3. *The creation of Mankind*

Day 7

And on the seventh day God ended his work which he had made; and he rested on the seventh day from all his work which he had made. And God blessed the seventh day, and sanctified it: because that in it he had rested from all his work which God created and made. (Genesis 2:2-3)

God rested from all His work that he had done on this day. There are inexhaustible truths and wisdom to learn from these six days of creation and one day of rest.

However, regarding *"planning,"* you can certainly learn to:

Decide what you want to accomplish

For each day, God had definite things that were accomplished in it. He knew exactly what He was doing. There was no trial and error. He had a design in mind because we hear this description during his daily work and at the completion of the work on Day six: *"And God saw everything that he had made, and, behold, it was very good" (Genesis 1:31).* The assessment of *"good"* or *"bad"* is not possible unless it is done against a standard or design.

Write it down

> *And the LORD answered me, and said, Write the vision, and make it plain upon tables, that he may run that reads it. (Habbakuk 2:2)*

Some have written regarding ideas or intentions, *"if it is not written down, it does not exist."* Once you have decided what you want to do, you have got to write it down.

Seeing your thoughts crystallised in writing harnesses your efforts toward the goals outlined in writing.

You cannot run unless you can see. If you are a driver, you will realise this interesting behaviour. If visibility drops suddenly as you drive, you will find that your foot will reflexively ease off the accelerator and locate the brake pedal to slow down.

Without thinking, you draw back on your rate of progress when you cannot clearly make out where you are going. Some of your delay comes from the hazy view of your goals. This lack of clarity may be primarily because they are not written down.

In the Old Testament, God would often speak to His servants and accompany His directives with the command, *"write it..."* We cannot be smarter than Him. Learn to do this in the small and you will be mindful to do it when it is most important. Take this for an example: if you cannot write down a simple grocery list, we cannot count on you to have a grocery budget. Your discipline in the least important or mundane of tasks will flow into your behaviour where it counts for more.

Divide the work into related sections or parts

The work allotted to each day was somehow related and could be classified into one day by some common characteristic. Doing this introduces some flow-logic to your work. One thing works into the next such that there is order in the progress of the tasks. When your work flows well from one thing to the next, the likelihood of re-doing is minimized.

Divide the work into time bound goals

Each section of the work of six days was allocated to a specific day. I do not believe that God was going to proceed into the next day before the plans for a particular day were accomplished. The end in sight was the seventh day as one of rest.

The law of God in making the seventh day Holy and a day of rest through Moses reveals how deliberate God is. With the seventh day in sight, every section of the work was to be done in its time.

Do the work that is required, one item at a time

Having allocated the work to be done in each day, what is clear is that all tasks were performed as planned.

We do not read that God met a hurdle and decided to postpone the task to another date. Our experience may most likely be different because God is perfect and we are only developing into His perfection. To complete assigned work in its time is the standard and goal.

However, you must do your best and migrate the spill over to the next allocated time.

To everything there is a season, and a time to every purpose under the heaven: (Ecclesiastes 3 verse 1)

There is a season and a time to every purpose and task. You must respect this and focus your attention on the things you have allocated to be done in that time. In view of this scripture, there may not be much wisdom in the way *"multitasking"* is commonly perceived as a virtue. This is debatable but all I can say is that we must be careful not to allow a lack of focus on defined tasks to compromise excellence.

Assess the work done for quality

We have mentioned earlier how God had a design. After the performance of your work, there must be a deliberate assessment of that work for the achievement of the objective or fitness to the design.

God's assessment of His work consistently came up with the result *"it was good"* because He is perfect, He makes no mistakes. Your assessment may not consistently yield this result; however, because you are made in His image, you will yield a good outcome more and more as you practice what you do.

Address any deficiencies in its quality

Where the outcome of the assessment of your work yields the result, *"it is bad or not so good,"* there is the need to address the areas where your work falls short. You are to do this until your work matches the design, desire or goal.

In conclusion, an excitable, party spirit overtakes people in the last three months of the year and especially in December. Even Christians have allowed themselves to be captured by this spirit in the name of Christmas and the New Year. You need to escape this blanket excitableness that makes people lose their direction and priorities. What sets December apart from March or any other month so that people should lose their minds?

Human tradition has been allowed to control people's lives. Don't get overexcited, whistle and scream when the clock chimes past midnight into a new year. A change on the clock does not imply a change in your life. You will fail in a new year just like you failed in the last if you do not become wiser. What can set a new year apart from an old one are the plans you make and how you follow them through.

"A CHANGE ON THE CLOCK
DOES NOT IMPLY A CHANGE
IN YOUR LIFE. WHAT CAN SET
A NEW YEAR APART FROM AN
OLD ONE ARE THE PLANS YOU
MAKE AND HOW YOU FOLLOW
THEM THROUGH."

8.

STRATEGY

Let us reiterate the place of planning. The purpose of planning in overcoming procrastination is to clarify your goals and objectives. When goals and objectives are well outlined, the fog clears and you are keener to act and make progress. We will talk about strategy in this chapter. Strategy is planning in-depth.

One may go further and develop a plan into a strategy by outlining:

1. *The Information required to achieve the goals*
2. *The People needed to assist in achieving the goals*
3. *The Things or Resources required*

Those that go to battle must first consider whether they can conquer with the resources available. This kind of planning to enumerate what is at your disposal increases your boldness. When you are bold, you move forward without hesitation.

These are the names of the men which Moses sent to spy out the land. And Moses called Oshea the son of Nun Jehoshua. And Moses sent them to spy out the land of Canaan, and said unto them, Get you up this way southward, and go up into the mountain: And see the land, what it is; and the people that dwell therein, whether they be strong or weak, few or many;

And what the land is that they dwell in, whether it be good or bad; and what cities they be that they dwell in, whether in tents, or in strong holds; And what the land is, whether it be fat or lean, whether there be wood therein, or not. And be of good courage, and bring of the fruit of the land. Now the time was the time of the first ripe grapes. So they went up, and searched the land from the wilderness of Zin unto Rehob, as men come to Hamath. And they ascended by the south, and came unto Hebron; where Ahiman, Sheshai, and Talmai, the children of Anak, were. (Numbers 13:16-22)

And they returned from searching of the land after forty days. And they went and came to Moses, and to Aaron, and to all the congregation of the children of Israel, unto the wilderness of Paran, to Kadesh; and brought back word unto them, and unto all the congregation, and showed them the fruit of the land. And they told him, and said, we came unto the land where you sent us, and surely it flows with milk and honey; and this is the fruit of it. Nevertheless the people be strong that dwell in the land, and the cities are walled, and very great: and moreover we saw the children of Anak there. The Amalekites dwell in the land of the south: and the Hittites, and the Jebusites, and the Amorites, dwell in the mountains: and the Canaanites dwell by the sea, and by the coast of Jordan. And Caleb stilled the people before Moses, and said, Let us go up at once, and possess it; for we are well able to overcome it. But the men that went up with him said, we be not able to go up against the people; for they are stronger than we. And they brought up an evil report of the land which they had searched unto the children of Israel, saying, The land, through which we have gone to search it, is a land that eats up the inhabitants thereof; and all the people that we saw in it are men of a great stature. And there we saw the giants, the sons of Anak, which come of the giants: and we were in our own sight as grasshoppers, and so we were in their sight. (Numbers 13:25-33)

When they reached the borders of the Promised Land, Moses could have commanded *"March forward and possess!,"* but he did not. Instead, he chose men to go and spy out the land first. Action should follow information. He had specific things that he wanted to know about, including the proof of the land's fruitfulness, *"and bring of the fruit of the land,"* he said. This is what he wanted to know:

1. *What is the land like?*
2. *Is it a good or a bad land?*
3. *Is the land fat or lean?*
4. *Is there wood in the land or not?*
5. *What are the cities like?*
6. *Do they live in tents or strongly built structures?*
7. *Are the people strong or weak?*
8. *Are the people few or many?*

"ACTION SHOULD FOLLOW INFORMATION"

With information at hand, Moses and his leaders could map out the strategy to possess. Again, just to reiterate the point, strategy is only a worthwhile engagement for someone who desires success. If Moses' attitude was *"alright, the Promised Land is before me, let's just see what happens,"* he would not have needed a strategy. The spies were sent out to obtain information sufficient to achieve success at what God had promised.

Taking inventory of the scale of the challenge or the strength of your enemy is not an engagement meant to intimidate you. This is where the other 10 spies failed. It is to inform you of the kind of spiritual and physical preparation necessary to overcome. Caleb got it right when he charged, *"Let us go up at once, and possess it; for we are well able to overcome it."* Consider how much faith Moses had. He had enough faith to continue leading a multitude of stubborn, complaining and doubting people for forty years without giving up.

This is how tenacious he was and yet within two months' journey (to and fro) of the Promised Land, he still demanded to get information before moving in. Research is not doubt, it is strategy.

"RESEARCH IS NOT DOUBT, IT IS STRATEGY"

Overcoming procrastination does not involve plunging without consideration. There is the *"wisdom of action"* that must be done. The wisdom of action includes planning and *"planning in-depth,"* Your chances of failure escalate with the amount of unplanned action you take. Planning is not delay or procrastination; it is part of the wisdom of action.

"YOUR CHANCES OF FAILURE ESCALATE WITH THE AMOUNT OF UNPLANNED ACTION YOU TAKE"

We do not act to fail, we act to succeed. To act without planning is a deliberate decision to fail outrightly or to have a mediocre outcome, both of which are failure.

For which one of you, intending to build a tower, does not sit down first, and counts the cost, whether he has sufficient to finish it? Lest, perhaps after he has laid the foundation, and is not able to finish it, all that behold it begins to mock him, Saying, This man began to build, and was not able to finish it. Or what king, going to make war against another king, does not sit down first, and consults whether he is able with ten thousand to meet him that comes against him with twenty thousand? Or else, while the other is yet a great way off, he sends an ambassador, and desires conditions of peace. (Luke 14:28-32)

The context of the above verse spoke of greater and deeper spiritual truths than mere *"planning,"* However, we do learn something powerful about the subject at hand. The Lord Jesus shows how it is clear that no one sensibly begins a building project before considering the resources at hand. Let us mine those verses line by line:

What is my goal?

"For which one of you, intending to build a tower...."

The clear visualization and crystallization of your goal is indispensable to strategy making. The goal is the reason for the formulation of strategy. Emphasizing the importance of goals was the purpose of the previous chapter and so I will not delve much into it again here.

Notwithstanding, it is important to reiterate this step as the foundation of strategy. The goal here is *"to build a tower."*

You must clearly see what you want to achieve and where you want to be when all is said and done. This is primary before we begin to discuss *how* to achieve the goal. The goal is the answer to the question *"what do I want to achieve?"* The strategy is the answer to the question *"how will I achieve it?"*

What does it take to achieve my goal?

".........does not sit down first, and counts the cost..."

With the goal firmly in mind, it is necessary to consider the resources required to achieve it. In both stories, the builder and the king, there is reference to *"...sit down first..." (v.28 and v.31)*. This is significant, inferring a seriousness of consideration of the matter. To *"sit down first"* speaks of a sober and disciplined effort. Dreams and goals are exciting; they give you wings for the sky. This is alright because that is the objective of a dream, a vision or a goal. It is an inspiration to help you go the distance. This is why at the prospect of a battle which an overconfident king may believe that he is certain to win, there is the advice to *"sit down first."*

This is needful planning in-depth. Determining that there is a worthy goal to be achieved is good but insufficient. To the outline of our goals, we must add a review of what is required to achieve them. Skipping this stage may make our goals only lofty ideals to which we are not prepared to assign the effort it takes to achieve them. Anybody can set a goal because anybody can dream. On the other hand, it takes a conscientious effort to climb down the high horse and consider the requirements of your dreams.

Vision, goals and dreams are the distant place we see when we ascend a high mountain and look out into the distance. There, in the heights, nothing is between us and our goals but space. As we stand there and look out into the distance with the wind in our face, we are tempted to believe that *"I will get there.....someday....it is only a matter of time."*

Strategy becomes a necessity when you descend the mountain peak and begin to walk the terrain in the valley. Now it is not space but rocks, cliffs, raging rivers, thorn bushes and thick foliage that stands as the challenge between you and the distant place you saw at the summit.

Face to face with the realities that oppose or separate you from your goal, you must consider the resources required to be successful. This is a necessary step to acting on what we desire to achieve.

Do I have enough to complete it?

".......whether he has sufficient (resources) to finish it" *(brackets mine)*

With a budget of the requirements for the fulfillment of the goal outlined, the next focus comes home. It is the honest appraisal of the time, resources and capabilities that we possess. This is what others call a *"reality check"* that many people may skip.

Attention that we place on ourselves may draw our attention to our weaknesses. Many of us do not enjoy this kind of attention on our frailties. Some consider it a lack of faith and would rather focus on their goals and move forward. Well, there is a difference between faith and presumption. Faith is not oblivious of the facts. It takes full consideration of the facts but denies their influence on the outome. Neither is faith blind. It has its eyes wide open, knowing what is present in the natural as well as what God has revealed in the spirit

"FAITH IS NOT OBLIVIOUS OF THE FACTS. IT TAKES FULL CONSIDERATION OF THE FACTS BUT DENIES THEIR INFLUENCE ON THE OUTCOME"

Refusing a self-assessment of this nature may be a choice not to act on your weaknesses, choosing to talk a good story that you consistently fail to achieve. This activity does not debilitate your faith by focusing on your weaknesses. On the contrary it gets your faith to work.

Faith has nothing to do in the absence of a challenge; indeed faith is useless unless there is human weakness. Remember the word of God came to Paul and said:

....My grace is sufficient for you: for my strength is made perfect in weakness.

Paul responded to this and said to us:

Most gladly therefore will I rather glory in my infirmities, that the power of Christ may rest upon me. (2 Corinthians 12: 9)

It is imperative to consider where you are now in relation to your goals and dreams. It is alright to see the gap. What you do on noticing that you do not have enough money, morality, education, influence, contacts or any other thing is the difference maker. Once you see your need, you must then exercise your faith and see God redeem you from your weakness.

For example, the first thing that a sinner must know is that he is a sinner. This fact does not need to paralyse a man. In light of the presence of the Lord Jesus Christ as saviour, there is hope that directs faith in a God that is able to alter that fact.

The same is true with any weakness or frailty you may identify in yourself. If we assume that the vision, goal or dream you have is God given and spiritual, we have to establish that it cannot be sick. God does not give lame or sick goals. On the other hand, *you* may be sick, unable, weak, faithless or poor because of this world. This is where you must respond and go to God and confess His word over your life. The scriptures have confirmed that even the poor and weak do not need to confess their condition; on the contrary, they are to confess their position in God. Let the weak *say* I am strong! *(Joel 3:10)*. The *fact* is *weakness*, the *faith* is *strength*.

It is important for you to consider whether you have the fortitude of character to take you where your dream is. Whether you have the moral excellence that is required to get and stay above. You must look and see whether you have the work ethic to be successful.

Where you are weak, begin to say that you are strong and act in alignment with what you said.

Do *now* what is required for you to arrive. Nobody got where they were going by standing still. You get *there* by walking *here*. Do it!

Take a look at these examples where there was an honest assessment of facts before faith was exercised in both speech and deed:

> *In the beginning God created the heaven and the earth. And the earth was without form, and void; and darkness was upon the face of the deep. And the Spirit of God moved upon the face of the waters. And God said, Let there be light: and there was light. (Genesis 1:1-3)*

There is no skirting about the matter here. Neither is there any *"positive"* but *"ignorant"* and *"presumptuous"* confession. There is an honest assessment of the situation as follows:

"And the earth was without form, and void; and darkness was upon the face of the deep."

This emptiness and darkness is not the close of the chapter because the very next verse shows us:

"And the Spirit of God moved upon the face of the waters. And God said, Let there be light: and there was light."

There is the presence and faithful words of God contrary to the facts that is confessed and acted upon.

"Let there be light," he says, to a place situated in darkness. Assess the facts but confess and act in accordance with the word committed to your heart and there will be a difference made.

And it was told the king of Egypt that the people fled: and the heart of Pharaoh and of his servants was turned against the people, and they said, Why have we done this, that we have let Israel go from serving us? And he made ready his chariot, and took his people with him: And he took six hundred chosen chariots, and all the chariots of Egypt, and captains over every one of them. But the Egyptians pursued after them, all the horses and chariots of Pharaoh, and his horsemen, and his army, and overtook them encamping by the sea, beside Pihahiroth, before Baalzephon. And when Pharaoh drew nigh, the children of Israel lifted up their eyes, and, behold, the Egyptians marched after them; and they were sore afraid: and the children of Israel cried out unto the LORD. And Moses said unto the people, Fear not, stand still, and see the salvation of the LORD, which he will show to you today: for the Egyptians whom you have seen today, you shall see them again no more forever. The LORD shall fight for you, and you shall hold your peace. And the LORD said unto Moses, Why do you cry unto me? speak unto the children of Israel, that they go forward: But lift you up your rod, and stretch out your hand over the sea, and divide it: and the children of

Israel shall go on dry ground through the midst of the sea.
(Exodus 14:5-7, 9-10, 13-16)

Earlier in this chapter, I said *"Faith has nothing do in the absence of a challenge; indeed faith is useless unless there is human weakness."* This is shown here clearly. There is no attempt to hide the strength of Pharaoh's army. There is even an enumeration of their might and we are told that Pharaoh brought with him *"six hundred chosen chariots."*

In the glare of the fact of the kind of arsenal that was coming against Israel, it is recorded that they *"were sore afraid"* and they *"cried out unto the Lord."* This was the response of their human nature to the strength of their enemy.

The answer was not in the fear of the human nature.

The answer as always lay in their reference to their confidence in God as Moses encouraged them, *"Fear not, stand still, and see the salvation of the LORD, which he will show to you today: for the Egyptians whom you have seen today, you shall see them again no more forever."* God does not expect you to close your eyes and act like you cannot see your challenges, weaknesses and incapacities. You must know and confront them with boldness and confidence that your opposition will be overcome by the power that God provides. There is no need to be paralysed from action because of challenges. Know the challenge, appreciate its strength and refer it to the Lord.

God did not falter in issuing his command and strategy in the face of an approaching enemy, *"Why do you cry unto me? speak unto the children of Israel, that they go forward."*

You are expected to act promptly to the instructions that God provides no matter what kind of opposition is against you. Had Israel failed to respond, they would have been destroyed and God would have been blameless.

And it came to pass, when David and his men were come to Ziklag on the third day, that the Amalekites had invaded the south, and Ziklag, and smitten Ziklag, and burned it with fire; And had taken the women captives, that were therein: they slew not any, either great or small, but carried them away, and went on their way. So David and his men came to the city, and, behold, it was burned with fire; and their wives, and their sons, and their daughters, were taken captives. Then David and the people that were with him lifted up their voice and wept, until they had no more power to weep. And David's two wives were taken captives, Ahinoam the Jezreelitess, and Abigail the wife of Nabal the Carmelite. And David was greatly distressed; for the people spoke of stoning him, because the soul of all the people was grieved, every man for his sons and for his daughters: but David encouraged himself in the Lord his God.

And David said to Abiathar the priest, Ahimelech's son, I pray you, bring me the ephod. And Abiathar brought the ephod to David.And David enquired at the LORD, saying, Shall I pursue after this troop? shall I overtake them? And he answered him, Pursue: for you shall surely overtake them, and without fail recover all. (1 Samuel 30:8)

When David and his men returned to Ziklag, they found their settlement burnt to the ground and their families captured. The situation is described clearly enough to comprehend. On appreciating these facts, the emotion of loss overwhelmed all the men and they cried until they had no more strength. There is clearly no denial of facts here. There is a clear reality check that shows what has happened.

David and his men do not stay in their wallowing because David led them out by encouraging himself in the Lord and enquiring as to what he must do. The Lord provides a response that gives strategic direction. This strategic direction can work in your life too by the ministry of the Holy Spirit to show you exactly what you must do to overcome the facts of your limitations.

"Pursue, overtake and recover all," is also true for you if you will allow the facts to work together to drive you to the Lord for the empowerment you need to overcome.

Can I go any further than the resources I possess?

"Lest, perhaps after he has laid the foundation, and is not able to finish it, all that behold it begins to mock him..."

Tangible and intangible resources are involved in getting things done. The tangible are the most obvious and intimidating, yet least important. The intangible are less obvious and ignored but are nonetheless the most important. It is obvious that we need *things* to get things done. Money, cars, houses, buildings, land, technology and books make the list. Access to these things is important to fulfill our goals.

On the other hand, the intangible of the fortitude of character, faith, time, spirit and prayer also make the list of resources needed to turn dreams into reality. These are ignored and yet are the pillars of accomplishment.

You can put millions of dollars in the hands of a man with poor moral fortitude and it is only a matter of time before he normalises the millions into an amount that his character can carry. Perhaps only thousands...or nothing.

Tangible or intangible, the words of the Apostle Peter to the lame man at the Beautiful gate ring true:

Then Peter said, Silver and gold have I none; but such as I have give I to you: In the name of Jesus Christ of Nazareth rise up and walk. (Act 3:6)

You can only give what you have. In the same way, you can only act and accomplish from what you have. Notice how the Lord said *"Lest, perhaps after he has laid the foundation, and is not able to finish it..."* In this example, the builder begins his project but is unable to complete it. He goes as far as to complete the foundation but this is as far as it goes because this is as far as the resources went. How far will your attitude and character take you?

Those who said *"your attitude determines you altitude"* were right, they had determined that you can only go as high and as far as the resources at your disposal can sponsor. We can easily appreciate that we can go no further than the fuel in a vehicle for instance. It is more difficult to accept that you can progress no further in life than the capabilities you allow God to build within you. There is a strategy required for where you are going. That strategy will say what skills, what knowledge, what time, what prayers, what character and all else that is required to get there.

"YOU CAN ONLY GO AS HIGH OR AS FAR AS THE RESOURCES AT YOUR DISPOSAL CAN SPONSOR"

These are key considerations that may account for your hesitation in the face of the things you desire to do. You will usually know it when you are neither ready nor capable to accomplish a thing. This does not mean that you need to be this way for good, however, recognising the fact of your present station and seeking to deal with that weakness conscientiously is a virtue.

What is the difference between glory and shame?

"......is not able to finish it, all that behold it begins to mock him..."

The difference between glory and shame is what you do. Having considered the race and the resources required to make progress, you must act promptly, otherwise you will not have a reward. Action is the last leg in the race. Having done all, you must still be found standing. The kingdom of God only has prizes for finishers. *(Ephesians 6:13, Galatians 6:9)*

If the goal is to complete the house and the builder falls short of it, shame becomes the outcome. Those who observe the matter will mock him. There is no glory before the finish line. This is why the identification of a goal is only a primary consideration. We must then develop a strategy to achieve it because the main thing is to get the goal accomplished.

"THE KINGDOM OF GOD ONLY HAS PRIZES FOR FINISHERS"

When you accomplish a goal, the result will be joy and God will be glorified. The joy and glory does not come from having a goal, a vision, an idea or a plan.

The joy comes from accomplishing it. The reason why a strategy must be considered is that it is impossible to cross the finish line and accomplish a goal when you are bankrupt of the resources and capabilities to do it.

This said, it is important for you to accept that after you have dreams, goals, plans and ideas, you are yet responsible for gathering the resources and capabilities required to fulfill them. These resources must be sufficient for the journey otherwise you may fail to start or collapse after only a few steps. When all is said and done, glory and the joy lies beyond the finish line, not a measure before it.

"AFTER YOU HAVE DREAMS, GOALS, PLANS AND IDEAS, YOU ARE YET RESPONSIBLE FOR GATHERING THE RESOURCES AND CAPABILITIES REQUIRED TO FULFILL THEM"

This *"planning in-depth"* helps you to act promptly and successfully on your goals. You cannot forego the setting of specific, time bound goals as well as the consideration of your readiness with the resources required and still be successful. When you succeed, you will find that success gives birth to more success because today's victory is part of the inspiration you need for tomorrow.

"GLORY AND JOY LIES BEYOND THE FINISH LINE, NOT A MEASURE BEFORE IT"

Remember *"Strategy,"* and in conclusion, look at the gospel text below, which could summarise the labour of this whole chapter:

1. *What is my goal?*
2. *What does it take to achieve my goal?*
3. *Do I have enough to complete it?*
4. *Can I go any further than the resources I possess?*
5. *What is the difference between glory and shame?*

And when they were come to the multitude, there came to him a certain man, kneeling down to him, and saying, Lord, have mercy on my son: for he is lunatic, and sore vexed: for oftentimes he falls into the fire, and often into the water. And I brought him to your disciples, and they could not cure him. Then Jesus answered and said, O faithless and perverse generation, how long shall I be with you? how long shall I suffer you? bring him here to me. And Jesus rebuked the devil; and he departed out of him: and the child was cured from that very hour. Then came the disciples to Jesus apart, and said, Why could not we cast him out? And Jesus said unto them, Because of your unbelief: for surely I say unto you, If you have faith as a grain of mustard seed, you shall say unto this mountain, Remove hence to that place; and it shall remove; and nothing shall be impossible unto you. However, this kind does not go not out but by prayer and fasting. (Matthew 17:14-21)

When a worthy challenge was brought before the disciples of Jesus, they could not handle it, though they tried. They had the desire to help just as they had witnessed the Lord Jesus do many times but could not give a victorious response. The wonderful thing about this particular incident is how the Lord Jesus clearly and unambiguously communicated the cause of the disciples' failure. Let us see how this account succinctly deals with the need to be strategic.

What is my goal?

The disciples' goal was to respond to the desperate man's call to help his son out of a recurrent and regular bondage. This is something that the disciples were most likely both willing and eager to do. I can reference a separate incident where the disciples were full of joy when they had achieved victory over unclean spirits *(Luke 10:17)*. They desired to help, and failed. *What are you desirous, willing and even eager to do?*

What does it take to achieve my goal?

The Lord Jesus responded to the disciples' enquiry for the reason of their failure by advising them that dealing with the unclean spirit required three things:

1. *Belief (faith)*
2. *Prayer*
3. *Fasting*

This was a straight forward, no-nonsense inventory of the resources required to achieve the task. This did not depend on who was involved, their level of education, history in the ministry or anointing. This was a neutral review of the scale of the challenge as it was. *What is the size of the challenge before you? What resources, spiritual and natural are required to move it?*

Do I have enough to complete it?

It is either you do or you do not. There is no middle of the road. If the challenge is going to move, there has to be sufficient resources available to do it. You cannot buy with less than the price marked on the product. The only exceptions are *"stealing"* or *"negotiating."* *"Stealing"* is out of the question so that leaves us with *"negotiating."*

Negotiation depends on the willingness of the other party to discuss. Evil spirits will not negotiate unless the other party is not negotiating. Some situations in life are like that, non negotiable, the price to accomplish the task just needs to be paid. You can expect a store to reduce its prices in a sale but the disciples could not count on the evil spirit lowering its stubbornness. *Are you ready to face your challenge?*

Can I go any further than the resources I possess?

You can count on the disciples' ability to answer this question promptly. They held the proof of experience that you *cannot* go any further than the resources you possess. It was clear the following had to grow in them to overcome the challenge:

1. *Belief (faith)*
2. *Prayer*
3. *Fasting*

How far can your current resources of moral fortitude, faith, prayer and discipline take you?

What is the difference between glory and shame?

A man comes to the Lord Jesus and at face value he may seem like one of the many who would throw themselves at the feet of the master for a solution. The man describes his situation and then hems it in with *"I brought him to your disciples, and they could not cure him."* This is what makes this scenario unique. This was the second time for this desperate man to relate the predicament of his household. The first time, he related it to *the willing* but *unable.* Now he related it to *the willing* and *able.* The ability of the Lord Jesus is distinguished from the inability of His disciples. His response shows it, *"O faithless and perverse generation, how long shall I be with you? how long shall I suffer you? Bring him here to me.*

"...bring him here to me" should have been the essential, confidence inspiring remark. I can picture the man getting quickly off his knees and rushing to pick up the boy. *"At last, a solution!"* he may have thought, with great joy!

A special note of the difference between glory and shame is the evident exasperation in the Lord Jesus' tone as he responds, *O faithless and perverse generation, how long shall I be with you? How long shall I suffer you? (endure your faithlessness and perversion) (Brackets mine).* This show of disappointment is suited to a teacher and master who clearly expected his pupils to be *"able"* by now but they failed. He still had to be the one to do what they ought to have attended to in his absence. Honour would have fallen on the teacher had he arrived and heard:

"Lord, *thank you!* My son: *was* lunatic, and sore vexed: for oftentimes he *used to* fall into the fire, and water. And I brought him to your disciples, and *they cured him.*

A *Strategy* demands that you pay attention to the resources required to complete an endeavour. Ignoring this is not faith. Things get done using things. You have to ensure you have everything you need for the journey. Some will be tangible, others intangible, but still required.

9.

PRIORITIES

As remarked earlier in *"Plan,"* the wisdom to be drawn from the creation text in the book of Genesis is inexhaustible. We learn more about the setting of priorities by several aspects of the process God followed during creation.

The setting of priorities is a subset of planning but is also worthy to stand alone for you to remember. When you have not identified what is most important for you to do, you may postpone the essential for the urgent and unimportant.

When you do this, you do not accomplish what is valuable to you. When you do not accomplish what is valuable to you, you do not solve your problems and add value to your life.

When you do not solve your problems and add value to your life you become inundated and overcome by life's challenges. When this happens, you spend most of your time dealing with the circumstances of life rather than making progress at what you are supposed to do, what you are called to do and your inner most desires.

Finding yourself in this place, you are frustrated, unhappy and dissatisfied.

In an earlier chapter, we referred to the words of the Lord Jesus Christ when His disciples offered him food at the well. The Lord Jesus said *"...my meat (satisfaction or fulfillment) is to do the will of Him that sent me" (John 4:34)*. It is no different with you. You will lack satisfaction and fulfillment when you do not do what is important. That which is important is God's will.

When you have come to a place of faith, God has put His will in your heart and your will and His are in alignment. When you do not do God's will, you are unfulfilled, miserable and feel worthless. God's will is the priority that all your life must focus upon and is the ultimate determinant of your sense of self worth.

We also looked at the book of Ecclesiastes which says, *"To everything there is a season, and a time to every purpose under the heaven" (Ecclesiastes 3:1).* We must know what we are supposed to be focused on at every stage of our lives.

Not all things are worthy of our attention.

We must be able to figure out what we are supposed to be doing amidst much that we *could* do. This is the place of priorities. We see this reflected symbolically in several ways which we can look at now.

Separate the needful from the needless

In the beginning God created the heaven and the earth. And the earth was without form, and void; and darkness was upon the face of the deep. And the Spirit of God moved upon the face of the waters. And God said, Let there be light: and there was light. And God saw the light, that it was good: and God divided the light from the darkness. (Genesis 1:1-4)

During creation, God separated the light from darkness. In the same way, we must separate what we must do from what we do not need to do. Take note that God separated *"the light"* from *"the darkness."* We will rightfully interpret the *"light"* as God's will and *"darkness"* as everything else. God's word says *"Thy word (will) is....a light unto my path" (Psalm 119:105) (brackets mine)*

The idea is to identify and separate your focus *from* everything else. By identifying your focus, and pulling it away from the clutter of life, the rest remains in its place, exposed for you to avoid. As an example, by identifying *"much prayer"* as your *"light"* or identified goal, you can pull it out from the rest of life's time-grabbers like *"much television."* You did not have to create a goal that says *"avoid much television,"* but as a matter of course, *"much prayer,"* leaves *"much television"* exposed for you to avoid.

In the first chapters of this book, we summarized the definition of *procrastination* as *"to postpone the needful for the needless."* Regarding television (TV), if you watched unproductive TV for an average of two hours a day for a whole year, you will have wasted as much as ninety full eight hour working days. In that time, you could be paid three months in salary or work eight hours daily for three months toward your goals. *"Unproductive TV"* is TV that does not add value to your goals. Your goals are *the needful* and any unproductive TV time is *the needless.* When you spend time on the needless, you have missed your priorities.

Identify what is at the top of your list

You need to set clear priorities, identifying what is at the top of your list, your chief aim. Setting what is at the top of your list is the first step to seeing what is second and third and so on.

God set the *"firmament"* (heaven) in position, whose place we know to be above. By deciding the position of heaven (above), there was an immediate division between that which is above heaven and that which is below it.

With any set of things that you have decided are worthy of your attention, there will be those things that are more important than others. This is an important thing to do because procrastination includes an unhealthy and prolonged preoccupation with tasks that are a part of the plan but not the priority.

No-one can make this decision for you. *You* need to do it. However, I will recap a concept I shared at the beginning to assist you:

We judge importance by the implications or impact of doing or not doing a thing.

It is the impact of leaving a task out completely that will help you determine its importance. Once you have decided this, it is important for you to stick to your priority list. The most important tasks are usually solutions to relatively large and complex problems.

Hard problems are not easy to solve and so it is natural human inclination to shy away from them and allow our attention to be taken with simpler albeit less important and so lower priority tasks.

This does not help you make progress. We make progress in life by establishing order and systems. In other words, *"by solving problems."* Tinkering about just doing anything is not necessarily *"working."* Solving problems is *"working."*

Another way of distinguishing high from low priorities is to consider which goals have an impact on the proper performance of others. For example, in baking, the task *"allow the cake to cool"* is a fore-runner to *"ice the cake."* If the cake is not allowed to cool, this will most likely affect the quality of the icing.

What will set you on course for failure downstream if you do not resolve it now? Act on those things now as a higher priority than others. You need to set yourself on course for success by doing the things that matter. Get it right, because *"heaven"* affects everything below it.

Do things within their time

Let us go further. The record shows us that the lights in heaven (the Sun, Moon and Stars) were *"for signs, and for seasons, and for days, and years..." (Genesis 1:14).* God set those big and smaller lights to be the distinctive marks and heralds of changing times and seasons.

To everything there is a season, and a time to every purpose under the heaven: (Ecclesiastes 3:1)

Specific things happen within seasons and every time within that season has a purpose. These are some of the principles of natural seasons and the same is true regarding *"the seasons of our lives."* It is important to understand what is at hand to be done in a particular time of your life. There are *two perspectives* I can point out regarding seasons and the things we are meant to achieve within them. These perspectives are key considerations for you to frame a correct and prompt mindset about acting on the things that God places on your heart to do.

Perspective One: There are things which are impossible to do in any other time but the present and appropriate.

A change in circumstances changes the landscape of your life. It is possible that many things you have the opportunity to do today and take for granted may become impossible for you to do in the future. For instance, there is the strength of youth which you may possess now to do many things in ministry to others, labour, commerce or other endeavour which because of a lack of strength, you may be incapable of doing in the future.

> **"MANY THINGS YOU HAVE THE OPPORTUNITY TO DO TODAY AND TAKE FOR GRANTED MAY BE IMPOSSIBLE FOR YOU TO DO IN THE FUTURE"**

A painful thing to experience is a present desire but absent ability. That combination of life will leave you grieved, frustrated and even bitter. This is a frustrating place and yet it may be better than lacking both *strength* and *desire*. Generally speaking, the youth have greater hope than the elderly. In youth, dreams are big and impossibilities are hard to appreciate. As time progresses, failure and nature take their toll and desire and dreams are diminished. There are things you must do now or it may become impossible to do them later for lack of *strength, desire* or both.

"THERE ARE THINGS YOU MUST DO NOW OR IT MAY BECOME IMPOSSIBLE TO DO THEM LATER FOR LACK OF STRENGTH, DESIRE OR BOTH"

Some things will be impossible to do for external and practical reasons like changes in society, laws and conditions that affect your endeavour. Some things you are interested in doing now will become the casualties of the progress of time and disappear. You are supposed to jump on them and do them now or their time will go with the season.

Let's look at commerce. There are industries that have totally transformed and the profitable of yesterday can hardly survive today. The printed Newspaper in Europe and the Americas has ebbed in profitability with more people consuming their content free or near-free on the internet. Traditional travel agencies have had to make way for online self service travel service providers. The fixed telephone line bowed to the mobile networks. This is proof that there is something that you are thinking of doing now, in this season which will be impossible to do in that format in the future. Do it now!

But exhort one another daily, while it is called Today; lest any of you be hardened through the deceitfulness of sin. (Hebrews 3:13)

For you know how that afterward, when he would have inherited the blessing, he was rejected: for he found no place of repentance, though he sought it carefully with tears. (Hebrews 12:17)

Perhaps the most serious example of impossibilities that flow from procrastination, deferment and misplaced priorities are what I am going to discuss now. When the Lord Jesus said *"I will never leave you nor forsake you,"* he meant it. He never will, but *we* may leave Him and forsake Him if we choose to. The Father will always forgive us for our sins. Yes, if we confess our sins and repent in the name of Jesus, we will be forgiven.

This is the point I want to make. The passage of time and the sin that develops in your heart carries the power to make it impossible for you to repent. The Father is always going to be on hand to forgive but it may become impossible for you to repent after a while. There is a deceitful power of sin that works in the heart progressively. Sin works on the heart, hardening it, making it progressively more difficult and ultimately impossible to repent.

"THE PASSAGE OF TIME AND THE SIN THAT DEVELOPS IN YOUR HEART CARRIES THE POWER TO MAKE IT IMPOSSIBLE FOR YOU TO REPENT"

Esau failed to *"(find a) place of repentance" (Brackets mine)*. God was there all the time, ready to forgive. Regrettably, crying and repentance are not synonymous. He cried but could not find a place of repentance. He tried to look for it but his heart remained in the same place, proud, justified in its ways and unable to change direction.

Perspective Two: There are things which would be best in the present and current season of your life and their importance is diminished with the passage of time until they are probably useless.

Your idea is needed to solve a problem today. Once a solution is acquired and published, your idea has lost its value. The value of your idea diminishes with the progress that is made to solve the problems that your idea is meant to address. You see how it can be possible for you to still do later what is in your heart to do today, yet it may have lost value? Anything worth doing must meet a need or solve a problem. This is what people pay for, the meeting of their needs and the resolution of their problems. If we assume that what you want to do solves a problem, it becomes obvious that you must do it in the season of the problem. If the need is solved, your idea becomes irrelevant.

"IF THE NEED IS SOLVED, YOUR IDEA BECOMES IRRELEVANT"

In those days came John the Baptist, preaching in the wilderness of Judaea, And saying, Repent: for the kingdom of heaven is at hand. (Matthew 3:1-2)

I indeed baptize you with water unto repentance: but he that comes after me is mightier than I, whose shoes I am not worthy to bear: he shall baptize you with the Holy Ghost, and with fire: (Matthew 3:11)

He must increase, but I must decrease. (John 3:30)

Take a look at John the Baptist's ministry. He was a trailblazer for the subsequent ministry of the Lord Jesus Christ. In terms of sequence, John's ministry would begin and that of the Lord Jesus would follow. The success of the ministry of the Lord Jesus Christ depended on the success of the ministry of John. If this was not the case, God would not have sent John. It was important for John to recognise his time and seize the day because soon the sun would set on his ministry and rise on that of the Lord Jesus Christ.

The ministry of John needed to *increase* in its time because there would be a time when it needed to *decrease*. In fact, when John's time was up, he was beheaded. His life was taken in the line of duty for the glory of God!

What are you waiting for? Recognise your season and time and do what needs to be done now. You will spoil or break the sequence if you are not prompt. There are conditions required by the next in line. Your timely work will create success for the next thing. Let your efforts add value to the purpose of the next assignment. Those efforts are not worthwhile outside their time.

Efforts are celebrated in the time they are needed.

There is a price to be paid for not paying attention to the timeliness of doing things

Agree with your adversary quickly, while you are in the way with him; lest at any time the adversary deliver you to the judge, and the judge deliver you to the officer, and you be cast into prison. Verily I say unto you, you shall by no means come out, till you have paid the uttermost farthing. (Matthew 5:25-26)

Things unattended get worse. The grass uncut will be longer tomorrow. The Lord Jesus teaches the same principle in the captioned text. The story set depicts the following characters:

- *The accused*
- *The adversary (someone with whom you have a dispute)*
- *The judge*
- *The officer (a prison official)*

The lesson is for us to learn the wisdom of *the accused* to work out a solution for a predicament promptly. In the story, if the accused does not negotiate with the adversary or opponent early, the situation gradually deteriorates. With time, the adversary may hand the accused over to the judge. The judge has no history of relationship with an accused person and will exercise his judgment on the facts, possibly without pity.

When the judgment is passed, the judge will hand the accused over to the officer. The officer's only instructions are to commit someone to the prison cell according to the judgment determined.

An example where the principles of this story usually work is the issue of debt. Debt strengthens its grip on a person with the passage of time. The individual or institution owed usually has a relationship with the debtor, otherwise there would have been no debt. The institution or individual owed represents the adversary. The best time to negotiate is when the matter is still with your adversary. You never know, perhaps they will have pity and extend the due date or better still, forgive the whole debt. If the owed gets fed up and hands over the matter to a judge, the debtor's fate may be sealed. In line with this story, the predicaments and problems in life will take a similar course, getting worse and worse with time, until it is nearly impossible for the one trapped to escape. Over time, escape may become impossible where it was previously only difficult and the concerned person refused to take on the challenge.

Procrastination is not only a delay of favourable outcomes; it results in a gradual decline in the chances of success. Act on it now. Challenges have the peculiar ability of graduating into a worse and bigger monster.

Kill it now, before it grows! If someone had killed Goliath before he was a full grown enemy giant, he would not have given an entire nation the jitters.

> *This know also, that in the last days perilous times shall come. For men shall be lovers of their own selves, covetous, boasters, proud, blasphemers, disobedient to parents, unthankful, unholy, Without natural affection, trucebreakers, false accusers, incontinent, fierce, despisers of those that are good, Traitors, heady, highminded, lovers of pleasures more than lovers of God; Having a form of godliness, but denying the power thereof: from such turn away. (2 Timothy 3:1-5)*

The above text is the testimony of a certainty. It will become more complex to preach the gospel. The answer is to preach as much and as far as we can in the time that we have now. Preaching the gospel now increases the foot soldiers on the ground so that more ground is covered against the perilous time to come.

Things will get more and more evil with time. A bad situation does not get better by leaving it the way it is. Those that are without Christ are essentially corrupted within. There is rottenness on the inside that requires the life of Jesus Christ to overcome. This corruptness or death will not get better without Christ. Time can only make the situation worse and the only intervention that will bring change is the gospel of Jesus Christ. If you were to pick up a rotten apple and see a worm wiggle its way into it, will that fruit become good by you putting it up in a safe, dry place and waiting? The answer is a resounding "No!" It can only rot further.

The preaching of the gospel of Jesus Christ is a key and important example of the price to be paid for not paying attention to the timeliness of doing things. Some places will be legally shut out from the public preaching of the gospel through the growing loving of pleasures and exclusion of God from the conscience of man.

Victory can only be decided by what we do now. Waiting is suicidal to our lives and mission. Set your priorities and do the things that matter now.

10.

DISCIPLINE & REWARD

Anything worthwhile will require some effort on your part to accomplish. This requires endurance and discipline. Pain is unpleasant and so it is something we will postpone for as long as we can get away with it.

We tend to postpone our pain. In doing this, we unwittingly postpone our reward. Again, this is a natural disposition which must be overcome by those who are spiritual. These are the two factors we want to explore, that is, *discipline* and *reward*.

> **"WE TEND TO POSTPONE**
> **OUR PAIN. IN DOING THIS**
> **WE UNWITTINGLY POSTPONE**
> **OUR REWARD"**

One of the foundations we want to lay in order to have total victory over delay is the principle of pain. There is a relationship between pain, suffering and resultant glory. This is true in a broad and great way as was accomplished by the suffering of the Lord Jesus Christ on the cross.

Without revelation, it would be impossible to recognise how something good could come out of the horrendous death of Jesus by crucifixion. He walked in dominion over sickness and death by healing the sick and raising the dead. Those who looked at Him seemingly helpless as he was led to His demise on the cross may have exclaimed, *"How are the mighty fallen?"*

This is the perception of the natural eye without the revelation of the glory that Godly suffering produces.

The writer of Hebrews attests to the insight and revelation that the Lord Jesus possessed as he went through the humiliating death of the cross.

Looking unto Jesus the author and finisher of our faith; who for the joy that was set before him endured the cross, despising the shame, and is set down at the right hand of the throne of God. (Hebrews 12:2)

The Lord Jesus Christ is the one who gave us the first fruits of what faith is. Not only that, He also completed faith, made it mature and handed it over to us a complete example.

The quoted verse describes how His faith behaved.

By reason of the joy that He perceived ahead of Him, He endured the gruesome pain of the cross. Imagine how much faith this was. The faith that the Lord Jesus proved on the cross was a real substance that offered a buffer between His painful body and soul experience and His inner spirit.

A man fails a matter when the spirit of faith in Him is too weak to carry the weight of a challenge. His faith cannot carry the situation, His mind gives up and everything else is a matter of course. His hands let go of the steering wheel as his foot eases off the accelerator pedal of life. He gives up and his life grinds to a sad halt... motionless, yet the bags were packed for the journey.

> ## "A MAN FAILS A MATTER WHEN THE SPIRIT OF FAITH IN HIM IS TOO WEAK TO CARRY THE WEIGHT OF A CHALLENGE."

The reward that Jesus perceived enabled Him to endure the pain that was necessary for Him to inherit it.

This was the cross of Jesus Christ and is not a far-fetched example. The principle is universal. Pain, suffering and discipline in the pursuit of a goal are the needful precursors of reward. The greater the discipline, the greater the reward.

For our light affliction, which is but for a moment, works for us a far more exceeding and eternal weight of glory; (2 Corinthians 4:17)

Paul says the above when dealing with the afflictions and sufferings of life which produce the power of God in ministers to bring grace to many through the gospel of Jesus Christ. He calls the troubles that are faced in this life *"light affliction..."* This is regardless of the extent to which many suffer in this life as they pursue righteousness. Paul still calls it *"light."* This is because lightness or heaviness are comparative terms. Light or heavy depends on *who* is carrying the object. For example, a brick may be *"heavy"* when picked up by a three year old and light when picked up by a fifteen year old.

In the quoted gospel text, the affliction is light in comparison to the *"....far more exceeding and eternal weight of glory."* The glory, benefit and reward far exceeds the trial and affliction that comes before it. This makes the affliction *light.*

Every goal to which we have been called by God requires the endurance of trial, affliction, hardship and labour. It is a spiritual principle which we do well to recognize and respect. The natural man will shrink at his goals on account of the work, trial and affliction related to their pursuit. The spiritual man should face the goal head on and as soon as required because of the reward he perceives. To wait is to waste opportunity and to turn back is to refuse the reward.

Where there is no vision, the people cast off restraint: but he that keeps the law, happy is he. (Proverbs 29 verse 18)

The absence of a clear vision and focus on the reward has the power to cause you to give up the discipline required to achieve your goals. At the beginning of this chapter, I said *"Anything worthwhile will require some effort on your part to accomplish."* Let us take a look at that word *"Worthwhile."* It is one of the fundamentals of discipline.

You have to determine that something is worth your while before you commit to it. Those two words put together are a treasure. What is the worth, the value, the reward for your *"while"*? You need to determine this correctly. What is the reward involved? What does it pay you? What is the desirable outcome from your efforts? Your *"while"* refers to the time and effort you will spend. After the reward is determined and it is favourable and desirable to you, yours is a conscious effort to pursue your reward with steely, unyielding determination.

There is no hidden agenda with God or in life. In almost every place where God requires obedience, he clearly outlines the reward. I will show you just three because *"...a three-fold cord is not quickly broken" (Ecclesiastes 4 verse 12)*

> *I call heaven and earth to record this day against you, that I have set before you life and death, blessing and cursing: therefore choose life, that both you and your seed may live: (Deuteronomy 30:19)*

> *Give, and it shall be given unto you; good measure, pressed down, and shaken together, and running over, shall men give into your bosom. For with the same measure that ye mete withal it shall be measured to you again. (Luke 6:38)*

> *But seek ye first the kingdom of God, and his righteousness; and all these things shall be added unto you. (Matthew 6:33)*

In the book of Habakkuk, there is the call to write the vision down and to make it plain in writing. The clear outline of goals is indispensable to the achievement of the things that you desire to do. We have discussed this in the chapter *"Plan."*

And the LORD answered me, and said, Write the vision, and make it plain upon tables, that he may run that reads it. (Habakkuk 2:2)

The outcome of having a clearly outlined vision or plan is that those that read it will *"run."* Note that the vision is to make the one who reads it *"run"* and not *"walk."* To *"run"* is an action that requires the application of discipline and effort in order to achieve desired results. Athletes apply discipline to their daily lives to win the races in which they compete. There is only a slight chance of winning races without discipline. That slight chance includes the possibility of racing against athletes who are as or more ill disciplined that you are. Life is rarely that benevolent.

The apostle Paul uses plain language when he discusses the example of the athlete in the book of *1st Corinthians* below:

Do you not know that they which run in a race run all, but one receives the prize? So run, that ye may obtain. And every man that strives for the mastery is temperate in all things. Now they do it to obtain a corruptible crown; but we an incorruptible. I therefore so run, not as uncertainly; so fight I, not as one that beats the air: But I keep my body under, and bring it into subjection: lest that by any means, when I have preached to others, I myself should be a castaway. (1Corinthians 9:24-27)

He first argues the fact that there are many who run in a race but only one wins, *"one receives the prize,"* he says. That is a simple yet profound truth. There is going to be a winner when all is said and done. Well, nowadays there can be a tie in some sporting disciplines, however, that tie could certainly be broken if enough time was spent on it. This would leave one emerging winner!

Paul then follows the certainty of a winner with the encouragement *"so run, that you may obtain."* In other words, *"live your life in a way that wins!"* This is remarkable. Paul desired his readers to win. The words he spoke and wrote were inspired by the Holy Spirit *(2 Timothy 3:16)* so God wants us to win! This lends further credence to our discussion in the chapter *"Your Success Is God's Will."*

The wisdom of God does not end at just encouraging us to win. The word of God goes on to show us *how* to win. Presented in my own words, Paul's message could be, *"Every man who is focused on becoming a master athlete must be disciplined in all things."* *"Every man,"* he says. Not *"some men."* That makes the statement a universal truth. Whoever is going to be a master athlete must follow the path of discipline. Avoiding the path can make you something else, but not a master athlete. Paul goes on to describe how the athletes apply themselves to such discipline in order to win natural accolades. He makes the comparison to show how those who are of faith should apply themselves to discipline much more in order to win spiritual accolades. Every plan will require discipline in order to *"run"* and fulfill it. The fulfillment of the vision or plan will always mean rewards to the runner and visionary.

With this background, we cannot afford to entertain the *"the leisure of laziness."* Laziness is that lack of energy that is overcome by a decisive discipline in life. Paul said he aims at his spiritual goals and runs with certainty by putting the *"body under."* This means to *"suppress the natural inclinations and appetites of the body in pursuit of a superior objective."*

"LAZINESS IS THAT LACK OF ENERGY THAT IS OVERCOME BY A DECISIVE DISCIPLINE IN LIFE"

The attitude adjusted by the background we have discussed so far in this chapter is the starting point to trump any tired feeling or condition in the body. Those feelings of fatigue will always get the better of you when they are accepted in your mind. It takes a well arranged series of excuses for your body to get the better of the right thing to do. Look at what the lazy man says in the scripture below:

The slothful man says, there is a lion outside; I shall be slain in the streets. (Proverbs 22:13)

The slothful man says, there is a lion in the way; a lion is in the streets (Proverbs 26:13)

What is that except a silly excuse? If laziness cannot get a valid reason to avoid the needful, it will find the most pathetic, baseless, senseless excuse. Laziness will go into the *"excuses database"* and pick out any reason it can use to postpone the needful and do the needless instead. This database exists in the mind of anyone who has not yet made the decision to delete it. Excuses are the scapegoats of the slothful. It is both shameful and heart rending for almost anyone who cares about success to admit that they are lazy. The usual way out is an excuse.

"EXCUSES ARE THE SCAPEGOATS OF THE SLOTHFUL"

Excuses empower doubt, unbelief and the realm of impossibilities. But this is not what you want for your life. You want to live in a realm of possibilities, where you do not hesitate to step out and do what God has placed on your heart to do. Remember that Jesus said to the desperate father:

..If you can believe, all things are possible to him that believes (Mark 9v23).

This is the mindset to keep, not the mindset that considers all the possible explanations, justifications and reasons why something cannot be done. Alright, so there will be justifiable reasons why you cannot do something immediately. However, you do not have to stay there. Consider the challenge and quickly work out a strategy to get it done. Never down your tools and go to sleep because of laziness. I figure if laziness was a person and walked the streets incognito, he would give himself away by his excuses.

The hand of the diligent shall bear rule: but the slothful shall be under tribute (Proverbs 12:24)

The complete opposite of laziness or slothfulness is diligence. Diligence is focused on doing whatsoever it is supposed to do, whether it feels good or not. The message does not come from the body when it comes to diligence, it comes from a made up mind. The reward of diligence is ruler-ship. This is dominion and leadership. Nobody wants to nor can be led properly by a lazy man. It is a complete disaster to be on a lazy man's ship.

He will decide to check his campus or GPS later, after his nap, sending everyone where they are not going!

This is the reason why the apostle Paul showed in his teaching that diligence was a key trait of leadership. Of all the characteristics he could have mentioned regarding leadership or ruler-ship, he wrote simply:

..He that rules, (must do it) with diligence (Romans 12:8) (brackets mine)

You cannot have God's blessing to be a leader and be lazy at the same time. There is no reward, prestige, honour or responsibility that God commits to the lazy. It may only be a little safer to have a lazy man only as a contributor, not a leader. In this case, when he does not feel like it, at least someone else can contribute and the ship does not have to head into the rocks. However, to have the leader of an endeavour lazy is a loss and danger to many.

There is responsibility, authority, gain and honour to the diligent and the opposite to the lazy. Discipline has made up its mind to do now what needs to be done, and earn its reward. Laziness has prepared reasons why it can only be done tomorrow, and becomes poor.

11.

THE HOLY SPIRIT

If you are born again according to our discussion in the second chapter, you are a candidate to receive the gift of the Holy Spirit. The Lord Jesus Christ promised to send the Holy Spirit to all who will believe. The Holy Spirit is the Spirit of our heavenly Father dwelling in you.

> *If you love me, keep my commandments. And I will pray the Father, and he shall give you another Comforter, that he may abide with you forever; Even the Spirit of truth; whom the world cannot receive, because it does not see him, neither does it know him: but you know him; for he dwells with you, and shall be in you. (John 14:15-17)*

When Peter preached the word as recorded in the book of Acts following the mighty outpouring of the Holy Spirit on the believers who were waiting expectantly, he made a wonderful remark.

> *Then Peter said unto them, Repent, and be baptized every one of you in the name of Jesus Christ for the remission of sins, and you shall receive the gift of the Holy Ghost. (Act 2:38)*

Why was it so important in the Heavenly Father's plan for humanity to send the Holy Spirit to dwell in us? The disciples did not wait fifty days for the day of the outpouring of the Holy Spirit to fully come for this to be done for no purpose. I will show you one all encompassing reason that we need the indwelling of the Holy Spirit in us. The word *"comforter"* there in *John 14:16* can also be rendered *"helper."* The Heavenly Father is dwelling in those who believe through His Holy Spirit because we need help. Just like the disciples needed to be with Jesus, we need the Holy Spirit with and in us to help us overcome in life.

> *Nevertheless I tell you the truth; It is expedient for you that I go away: for if I go not away, the Comforter will not come unto you; but if I depart, I will send him unto you. (John 16:7)*

The Lord Jesus spoke to the disciples and showed them that the Holy Spirit would come in His place to do more than what He did when He was with them. The word *"expedient"* there means, *"to your advantage."* The Holy Spirit would come to do *more* otherwise there would be no advantage.

The Holy Spirit would not come while Jesus was still with the disciples because he was playing the part that the Holy Spirit would come to fulfill. Jesus was a helper, a support and source of empowerment for His disciples. However, His ministry and support to them was limited and confined to the places He was physically. When He was with them, He could teach them, encourage them and direct them. When he was far from them, they had to depend on what they could remember. This is the advantage that the Holy Spirit would bring. He would be a source of power, teaching and direction *personalized and indwelling* each disciple of Jesus Christ.

The gift of the Holy Spirit was promised to every single person that is born again. This was the Apostle Peter's message to the multitude in *Acts 2:38* and is a message to us all today. The same faith that causes you to be born again is the same faith that causes you to receive the gift of the Holy Spirit.

And be not drunk with wine, wherein is excess; but be filled with the Spirit; Speaking to yourselves in psalms and hymns and spiritual songs, singing and making melody in your heart to the Lord; (Ephesians 5:18)

It is good but insufficient to receive the gift of the Holy Spirit and leave it there. There is your responsibility as a believer to ensure that you remain filled with the Holy Spirit. The Lord Jesus promised that the Holy Spirit will live with us forever in the gospel of John. This is true; He will never leave us nor forsake us. However, it is a decision of discipline to determine at what level you keep your "cup," at the bottom, in the middle, at the brim or overflowing.

You can remain filled with the Holy Spirit by keeping your attention fixed on the Heavenly Father, worshipping him, singing and joyful by faith in the name of the Lord Jesus Christ.

And they of the circumcision which believed were astonished, as many as came with Peter, because that on the Gentiles also was poured out the gift of the Holy Spirit. For they heard them speak with tongues, and magnify God. Then answered Peter, Can any man forbid water, that these should not be baptized, which have received the Holy Spirit as well as we? (Act 10:45-47)

When you receive the gift of the Holy Spirit, you will receive a special and heavenly language. Speaking in tongues keeps you filled with the Holy Spirit. When you are in that condition, you are ready for action. You are ready to obey the promptings of the Holy Spirit, doing what you are directed to do.

The Holy Spirit is your Heavenly Father working in you as a power agent of action. When you are filled, you will do because your Heavenly Father is a doer. Being either empty or with just a stagnant well of the Spirit limits you to have your destiny confined to the limitations of your nature. Your nature refers to the natural tendencies of life such as, to be afraid, to be lazy, to be intimidated by others or to lack confidence in your abilities. All this is overcome by the Holy Spirit. There is no shortcut. To be filled with the Spirit is the way to be a doer.

And Jesus came and spoke unto them, saying, All power is given unto me in heaven and in earth. Go therefore, and teach all nations, baptizing them in the name of the Father, and of the Son, and of the Holy Ghost: Teaching them to observe all things whatsoever I have commanded you: and, look, I am with you always, even unto the end of the world. Amen. (Matthew 28:18-20)

"THE HOLY SPIRIT IS YOUR HEAVENLY FATHER WORKING IN YOU AS A POWER AGENT OF ACTION"

And, being assembled together with them, commanded them that they should not depart from Jerusalem, but wait for the promise of the Father, which, he said, you have heard of me. (Act 1:4)

But you shall receive power, after that the Holy Ghost is come upon you: and you shall be witnesses unto me both in Jerusalem, and in all Judaea, and in Samaria, and unto the uttermost part of the earth. (Act 1:8)

The Lord Jesus said to the disciples in my re- phrasing, *"go...but wait...until you are filled."* Well, you will not find a verse that says that but a combination of the verses captioned above gives you that message. He commissioned them to action as recorded in *Matthew 28:18-20* and yet tells them to wait and not act on His command until they receive the power.

This shows me that the Holy Spirit's power is the determinant of success. It is the power to overcome every single hindrance to the success of the mission commissioned in *Matthew Chapter 28.* In all of life, there is no bigger assignment than the assignment given by the Lord Jesus Christ in *Matthew Chapter 28*. All the assignments of this world put together do not compare to the assignment of winning the souls of men for God.

If the power of the Holy Spirit was the answer prescribed for the greatest, the most important, most urgent task in the world, He is the answer for every other mission in this world. The Holy Spirit ensures that every challenge, in whatever form it may present itself is overcome.

"THE HOLY SPIRIT'S POWER IS THE DETERMINANT OF SUCCESS"

And now, Lord, behold their threatenings: and grant unto your servants, that with all boldness, they may speak your word, By stretching forth your hand to heal; and that signs and wonders may be done by the name of your holy child Jesus. And when they had prayed, the place was shaken where they were assembled together; and they were all filled with the Holy Spirit, and they spoke the word of God with boldness. (Acts 4:29-31)

The apostles of Jesus Christ, including Peter were threatened by the scribes, rulers and elders of the temple for preaching the gospel of Jesus Christ. Powerful people in the establishment of their day had arisen to hinder their assignment. The apostles did not scurry into hiding like frightened puppies. The bible says in *Acts 4:24*, "... *they lifted up their voice to God with one accord..."*

The answer to their challenge was with God and what they did was to lift up their voices and pray to Him for that solution. They prayed concerning the hindrance and threat to their ministry. Their prayer was good but it is the response to their prayer that is most interesting to me. God did not bring down fire and consume their opposition. The captioned verse records that the place was shaken in response to their prayers and they *were all filled with the Holy Spirit*. To deal with their opposition, God acted on the apostles, not on the opposition. However, by filling the apostles with the Holy Spirit, he was dealing with their opposition. From that moment, they got up and continued to speak the word of God with boldness, regardless of what the priests had said.

Hesitation comes from emptiness. When you are filled with the Holy Spirit, you will move forward. This is just like a car with a tank full of fuel will not *hesitate* to move forward when the accelerator is pressed.

"HESITATION COMES FROM EMPTINESS"

To receive and be filled with the Holy Spirit is the underlying and most important factor in every piece of wisdom we have shared about overcoming procrastination. Without the Holy Spirit, it is mere human effort and that is critically limited. With everything that a person can do without faith in God, they still miss out on God's best. It is the Holy Spirit who knows the way to God's best. Believe, receive and be filled with the Holy Spirit through faith in Jesus Christ.

"TO RECEIVE AND BE FILLED WITH THE HOLY SPIRIT IS THE UNDERLYING AND MOST IMPORTANT FACTOR IN EVERY PIECE OF WISDOM WE HAVE SHARED ABOUT OVERCOMING PROCRASTINATION"

12.

NOW IS THE TIME!

Now is the time to act on all that God has placed upon your heart to do. Do not wait. Grow by doing. To pray, plan, and gather your facts is to act too. Do it! As you go, remember these things:

1. *If you do not have goals then you have nothing to pursue. Your life is either at a standstill or it is being spent on a wasted effort. Pray if you do not have goals. The Holy Spirit will give you enlightenment.*
2. *If you have goals but are hesitant because of doubt and fear then your recourse is again to prayer and the word of God, to establish the spirit of faith. Faith cannot be obtained when you are out of alignment with the will of God. To grow your faith is to clarify the will of God.*
3. *If you doubt your abilities, get into the word of God and prayer! If God has placed it upon your heart, use what you have and your abilities will grow. Growth comes from use and faithfulness. You have no excuse.*
4. *If you want to act now but it looks too big and you do not know where to start, be calm. Sit down with pen and paper and plan. Decide what the most important things are. Decide what is at the top of the list and what is second, third and so forth will fall into its place. Break the meal into small pieces*

and bite what you can chew. Chew and swallow then pick up the next piece. Rushing may choke you.

5. *If your mind shrinks at the work involved, remember the reward. To shrink from the task is to shrink from the reward.*

From now on, make a deliberate and resolute decision to do immediately that which must be done, even to the most minute of the tasks of life. When you use something, put it back where it must be. Do it now, not in thirty minutes. Clear your food plate to the kitchen, do it now, not after the TV show. Clear your clothes to the wash as soon as they come off your body, your shoes to the rack as soon as they come off your feet. Do not leave them in a pile where your feet were as though you have been abducted by aliens. Train yourself in the small and you will be ready for the big.

"WE CANNOT AFFORD TO DELAY IN OVERCOMING DELAY"

www.ingramcontent.com/pod-product-compliance
Lightning Source LLC
Chambersburg PA
CBHW061731020426
42331CB00006B/1193